CHINESE TREATIES
The Post-Revolutionary Restoration
of International Law and Order

by GARY L. SCOTT

1975
OCEANA PUBLICATIONS, INC. — DOBBS FERRY, NEW YORK
A. W. SIJTHOFF — LEIDEN

Library of Congress Cataloging in Publication Data

Scott, Gary L 1937-
    Chinese treaties.

    Bibliography: p.
    Includes index.
    1. China--Foreign relations--1949- 2. China--
Foreign relations--Treaties. I. Title
JX1570.S35   341.3'7'0951   75-14238
ISBN 0-379-00415-1   (Oceana)
ISBN 90 286 02259   (Sijthoff)

Manufactured in the United States of America

TO

EUGENE EMERSON SCOTT

Father. . .Friend

PREFACE

Treaties constitute the principal means by which
the People's Republic of China establishes and carries
out its external relations. In this respect the PRC
does not differ from most of the other nations of the
world. In light of the PRC's revolutionary nature,
however, little confidence has been displayed by outside observers in her willingness and ability to separate revolutionary rhetoric from stable practice in
the matter of international relations. This study
combines both quantitative and qualitative treaty data
in an attempt to demonstrate that PRC practice in
international relations does not differ distinctly
from the practice of most nations of the world.

The study also attempts to establish a "hard
data" base by which the People's Republic of China
can be compared with other States on questions other
than the "normalcy" of her international relations. The
availability of quantitative treaty data for the international community as a whole has made it possible to
compare PRC treaty patterns with those of other States,
groups of States and the world as a whole. Through
the use of these combined data this study hopes to
introduce another important indicator of the politics,

attitudes and actions of the PRC in the international system.

In the course of this study there have been many individuals who have aided me in seeing it through to its completion. Since there have been so many, whose assistance has ranged from substantive suggestions to warm encouragement, and since I do not wish to slight anyone, I would like to express my thanks collectively to all who have aided and encouraged me in this project.

I would like to single out a few individuals whose assistance was especially beneficial to me at critical times. I wish to extend my thanks to Anabel and Oscar Bentson, whose technical assistance, encouragement and occasional meals proved invaluable in the completion of the project. My very special appreciation and gratitude must go to Peter H. Rohn for his encouragement and assistance from the very beginning of this project. There is little doubt that without his suggestions and criticism of earlier drafts, this project might not have reached it completion. I am indebted to Nancy Gustafson, who typed the final manuscript, and who assisted greatly in its overall final preparation. Virginia Harrison shared the burden of indexing. The much needed funds for secretarial assistance were provided through a research grant

by Carleton College.

    Finally, a special acknowledgment is due my wife,
Karen. Her love, encouragement, willing assistance
and ability to create an overall happy environment
was the _sine_ _qua_ _non_ for the completion of this book.

GARY L. SCOTT

LIST OF TABLES

ABBREVIATIONS

The following abbreviations have been used in the footnotes and text to denote treaty series and collections and also to simplify the references to Chinese Language materials.

ILM	International Legal Materials
JMJP	Jen-min jih-pao (People's Daily) Peking
KCWTYC	Kuo-chi wen-t'i yen-chiu (Studies in international problems) Peking
KMJP	Kuang-ming jih-pao (Enlightenment Daily) Peking
LNTS	League of Nations Treaty Series
NCNA	New China News Agency
SCMP	Survey China Mainland Press, U.S. Consulate, Hong Kong
TWKH	Chung-hua jen-min kung-ho-kuo tui-wai kuang-hsi wen-chien chi (Collection of documents relating to the People's Republic of China) Peking
TYC	Chung-hua jen-min kung-ho-kuo t'iao-yueh chi (Collection of Treaties of the People's Republic of China) Peking
UNTS	United Nations Treaty Series

TABLE OF CONTENTS

Chapter

CHAPTER I

INTRODUCTION

> In the first place there is the inher-
> ent importance of the subject. The law of
> treaties, the law of contracts to use the
> common law term, the law of obligations to
> use the civil law term, constitutes the [1]
> very heart of any coherent legal system.

The People's Republic of China (PRC) since its

inception in 1949 has constituted a major factor in

world affairs. Logically classified as both a new

State (or at least a new government) and a Socialist

State, the PRC exhibits similar propensities toward

the reliance on treaty relations as do the other new

and Socialist States. In fact, so great is the PRC's

reliance on this means of establishing and carrying

out its external relations that it ranks among the

world's leaders in volume of treaties concluded.[2]

There are, of course, many indices of a State's

actions on the international scene. Among them are

trade figures, political literature, both official and

unofficial, communications data, foreign aid data and

international agreements. The following study will

analyze the international agreements of the People's

Republic of China as a specific indicator of that

country's politics, attitudes and actions in the in-

ternational system.

1

It hardly need be said that any single indicator
of a State's interactions with other States cannot
serve as a total representation of that Nation State's
proclivity to specific kinds of actions and reactions.
What can be said, however, is that a consolidation of
in-depth studies of the various indices of international behavior can serve to formulate a clear analysis of any Nation State's behavior vis-a-vis other
Nation States.[3]

This study will attempt to add to the existing
body of knowledge still another viewpoint from which
the People's Republic of China may be examined and
compared with other States in the international system.
In view of the increasing importance of treaty relations in the international system, it is felt that the
study of the treaty practices of the PRC is an extremely important addition to this body of knowledge.

Other quantitative data compiled on the PRC will
be used in this study in order to demonstrate that the
treaty relations of the PRC, like those of any other
country in the world, are a meaningful addition to the
realm of comparative information. Since information
of this nature gains its full value from a comparison
with the same type of information about other countries, this study will compare and contrast the PRC's
treaty patterns with other individual States, blocs

and the world as a whole.

Treaties as Data

The conduct of international relations, and the
set of rules for the governance thereof, have increasingly, since the middle of the nineteenth century,
come to be dependent upon the execution of international bilateral and multilateral agreements known
by the generic term "treaties."

Economic arrangements between nations such as
trade and aid are actualized by means of treaties.
International organizations and alliances are formed
through the use of treaties. The Charter of the United Nations is itself a treaty acceded to by all member nations. Recognition of States, diplomatic exchanges and privileges, the law of the sea -- virtually all dealings between and among States are brought
about and regulated by means of some form of treaty.
Even regulations concerning the conduct of war and
the establishment of the new status quo following a
war is done by treaty.

As a "source" of international law, treaties
have taken a preeminent place among the various sources recognized under traditional Western international law. Article 38 of the Statute of the International Court of Justice in listing the various
sources of law which the Court is instructed to apply

in the settlement of disputes lists "international conventions, whether general or particular," as first
among four recognized sources. Second in the listing
is "international custom."[4]

In addition to the rather subtle qualitative
shift toward dependence upon treaties as a source of
law, there has been a dramatic shift in sheer volume
of treaties, especially since World War II.[5] Since
the beginning of the United Nations over 10,000 treaties have been registered with that body in accordance
with Article 102 of the Charter.[6]

Since 1958, as a result of the codification by
treaty of both the law of the sea and the law of diplomatic and consular relations, the bulk of day-to-
day international relations is now governed by treaty
and not by international custom.[7]

The shift from reliance on customary international law to the reliance on treaties for the regulation of State interaction is not an altogether surprising occurrence. The explanation lies in part with
the great proliferation of new States since the founding of the United Nations. In a period of a quarter
of a century the number of independent sovereign Nation States in the world has increased nearly three-
fold. The original U.N. membership of 45 in 1946 had
increased to 132 by 1972. With all of these new

States entering into treaty obligations among themselves and with already established States, they have
accounted for a considerable share of the increase in
treaty frequency.

This then, in part accounts for the tremendous
increase in numbers of treaties. But what of the qualitative increase in the reliance on treaties as a
source of international law? Again it is possible to
turn to the newer nations for part of the explanation.
These new States, having recently thrown off the bonds
of colonialism, have been reluctant to accept anything that can be classified under the general rubric
of "colonial inheritance." Since the new States feel
that they had nothing to do with the establishment of
customary international law, they view such rules as
falling within this general category and are thus unwilling for the most part to be bound by them.[8]

Since rules made by treaty are a result of an
agreement between two or more States and since it is
clear that no State can be bound without its consent
by a treaty to which it is not a party,[9] new States
view this form of regulation of international conduct
as most compatible with their interests.

Another factor in the increased reliance on treaties is the attitude of the Socialist States toward
treaties and customary international law. The Soviet

Union, for example, while not totally disregarding the validity of international custom as a source of international law, nonetheless regards treaties as constituting, "...the main source of International Law."[10] The reasons behind this attitude by the Soviet Union and other Socialist States are similar to the reasons underlying the attitudes of the new States in general.

Finally, there is a logical reason for an increased reliance on treaties for the governance of international relations. Given the lack of a <u>universally</u> accepted body of customary rules in international law it seems natural that in an increasingly complex world there is a need to turn to the more concrete and definitive rules established by treaties.[11] International custom, while certainly not without importance, cannot hope to be as flexible and as rapidly adaptive to the frequent shifts in the international system as law established by treaties.

Treaties may be examined from several viewpoints. They can be treated as a sort of official literature of the country and a textual analysis made of them. Treaty language may often times be more reliable than the normal government communiques regarding States' attitudes toward the international environment. Treaties are, by definition, agreements or contractual arrangements between two or more parties and therefore

presumably are expressions of mutual consent to carry out specific actions. Moreover, treaty language is usually regarded by States as a reasonably precise expression of another State's will vis-à-vis a particular situation.[12] Treaties may also be examined in an historical framework, selecting and concentrating on those treaties that seem most important in any given historical period.

The quantitative approach to the examination of Chinese treaties will be used here in order to establish a framework of "hard" data within which one may work in making certain assumptions about Chinese foreign policy practices. Though until recently the study of treaty magnitudes and trends has been almost totally ignored, and though there are of course some inherent weaknesses in any quantitative study, magnitudinal studies of treaty relations have nonetheless proven to be of considerable value.[13]

Since it is now possible with the aid of computers to establish the quantity, distribution and trends of treaties, this information need not be overlooked in formulating hypotheses concerning a State's foreign policy. For example, one would want to think twice about attempting to show that trade relations are determined by ideology if the largest volume of trade treaties happen to be with ideologically op-

posed nations. At the very least it gives a new dimension to the problem that must be dealt with before the analyst can be certain of his conclusions.

Sources

The data base for this study is a subjective selection of 1,660 bilateral treaties of the People's Republic of China from several sources including the official PRC treaty series[14] and the monumental work of Douglas M. Johnston and Hungdah Chiu, Agreements of the People's Republic of China, 1949-1967: A Calendar.[15] The term "treaties" is used in the generic sense and includes all such instruments regardless of title, i.e. treaties, agreements, protocols, exchanges of notes, accords, contracts and others.[16] The selection of treaties was made using as nearly as possible the criteria which would make the treaty eligible for entry into the United Nations Treaty Series (UNTS) as a separate document.[17] Generally speaking it is the more formal and "original" documents which have been included. That is to say that protocols, exchanges of notes and other less formal arrangements which merely supplement, prolong or amend existing agreements have been excluded.[18]

There is a dual purpose in these criteria. The first is that by selecting the more formal documents, the chances for more complete information are greatly

increased over a study which would attempt to include
all existing international arrangements.[19] Second,
since the value of a study of this type derives from
its comparability with other similar data concerning
other States, and since the only comprehensive data
base of world-wide treaty patterns which presently
exists covers the UNTS, every effort was made to select
data as nearly comparable to the UNTS base as possible
without distortion.

This selection yields a total of 1,660 PRC treaties for the present study. This is less than is included in the Johnston and Chiu Calendar[20] (1,925 bilateral agreements), but more than the 770 bilateral
agreements included in the official PRC treaty series
(TYC).[21] Two reasons account for the low number of
instruments listed in the TYC. The most obvious is
that the series is complete only through 1964. The
other reason is that many important agreements shown
in the Johnston and Chiu Calendar and various other
sources have not been included in the TYC. This may
seem surprising at first. In fact one author has com-
mented on the possible legal significance of this fact
in the following manner:

> ...many of the CPR's agreements are not pub-
> lished in the official T'iao-yueh chi (TYC....
> It is obscure what legal distinction exists,
> if any, between treaties and agreements repor-
> ted in the TYC and those that are not.[22]

It is suggested here that we should not try to attach legal significance where most likely none exists. It can be shown that the absence of treaties from a country's own official treaty series is not at all an unusual occurrence.[23]

A survey of national treaty series of various countries will show that even Western countries are lax at registering treaties in the UNTS and/or their own national records, in spite of the United Nations Charter provision which calls for registration of all treaties entered into by its members.[24] For instance, Canada and Turkey have only about 75% and 65% of their nationally recorded treaties in the UNTS,[25] and, conversely, Norway has 136 treaties registered in the UNTS that do not appear in Norway's own official treaty series.[26]

Necessarily in a subjective selection of data of this sort, the question of distortion arises. Trends and magnitudes will be affected if the magnitudes of the selected base are not comparable with the total base. Table 1 shows the annual magnitudes of the Johnston and Chiu Calendar (complete through September 1967) compared with those of the current study. The two curves are strikingly similar. Therefore, what little distortion the final results may have on this count should be negligible. The Chinese treaty

series is not shown due to the relative paucity of
that collection for reasons previously stated.

Quantitative treaty data for all countries except
the PRC was provided by the computerized data bank of
the Treaty Research Center at the University of Washington.[27] Substantive treaty information from the
texts of PRC treaties was taken from the official PRC
treaty series (TYC) and from English translations appearing in the UNTS and various other sources.

In addition to the quantitative data base, the
theoretical and legal material used in the analysis of
Chinese treaty relations has been drawn from several
areas. Material used for the comparison of PRC legal
attitudes and practices with those of other States has
been drawn primarily from Western international law
materials, particularly the ILC Draft Articles on the
law of treaties and the Vienna Convention on the Law
of Treaties. Of particular help in the analysis of
these materials was Rosenne's The Law of Treaties.[28]
For comparison with Soviet treaty practices Triska
and Slusser's notable work has proven invaluable.[29]

Since mid-1971 scholarly interest in the PRC has
been heightened by two major events concerning that
nation's role among the nations of the world.

On October 25, 1971 the People's Republic of
China by a vote of the General Assembly of the United

TABLE 1

PRC BILATERAL TREATY FREQUENCY

- - - - Johnston and Chiu Calendar bilateral treaties

——— Selected Bilateral treaties included in this study

Nations was given the seat formerly held by the Republic of China in the U.N. General Assembly and Security
Council.

In February 1972 the President of the United
States made an unprecedented visit to the PRC to meet
and talk with Chairman Mao-Tse-tung and Premier Chou
En-lai. This visit was billed as a gesture of friendship and was one of the first signs of de facto recognition given the PRC by the United States.

There has always been interest in China, but
these two major events sparked new interest in business, legal and academic circles alike. Interest has
been especially high regarding China's international
dealings and Chinese attitudes and practice in both
municipal and international law. As a result there
have been numerous studies published in recent months
concerning these areas of Chinese affairs.[30] This
spate of literature on law and the PRC has aided the
author greatly in the legal and theoretical analysis
of the quantitative data. Special mention should be
made of the extremely important new two volume work
by Jerome Cohen and Hungdah Chiu on the subject of
China and international law. This documentary study
has, as the author's intended, made available "in con-
venient form the PRC's views on the entire spectrum of
questions ordinarily encompassed by that subject."[31]

The availability of translations of original PRC documents in collected form should greatly facilitate future research in this area.

It should be noted here that there is an extreme
paucity of international legal material written by
scholars and practioners within the PRC itself. Most
of the material that is available is dated since the
supply of material prior to the Great Proletarian
Cultural Revolution was very limited and since there
have been no PRC publications on international law in
the post-Cultural Revolution period.

Methodology

This study will utilize, in part, the traditional
methods for analyzing treaty practices, such as textual analysis of the treaties of the PRC (in so far as
texts or translations thereof are available) and the
consideration of available theoretical and legal literature on specific treaties and treaty practices.
This method of analysis will provide the kind of
"treaties as official literature" approach mentioned
above.

The major portion of this study will diverge
from these traditional methods in the use and consideration of quantitative treaty data. Quantitative
analysis will be used to locate discernible trends
and patterns in PRC treaty practice. Treaty data

will be considered <u>in toto</u> as well as categorically.
The value of these types of data is that they allow
comparative analysis to be made on treaty practices,
both totally and categorically, with any other single
nation, group of nations or the world as a whole.
This type of comparative analysis is useful in attempting to ascertain exactly how closely the PRC resembles the Western norm as a treaty maker.

Additionally, only through the use of quantitative data can the effects of various internal and external economic and political events on treaty-making
accurately be determined. Correlational analysis of
economic and political trend and events data combined
with quantitative treaty data should give a far more
accurate picture of the kinds of phenomena most af-
fecting treaty trends than heretofore provided by traditional methods of analysis.

The analysis of these data when combined with the
traditional methods of treaty analysis should give a
more in-depth view of the treaty practices of the
People's Republic of China than is possible by the use
of any single method of analysis.

Historical Background

The focus of this study is on the People's Republic of China, a government that has been in control of
mainland China only since the consummation of the rev-

olution in 1949. China is, of course, an ancient civ-
ilization, dating many centuries old, richly steeped
in tradition and culture. In spite of the revolutionary nature of the Communist Chinese regime and
their proclaimed adherence to the principles of
Marxism-Leninism and the Thought of Mao-Tse-tung, it
is felt by many scholars concerned with China that the
Chinese Communists have not been able to free themselves entirely from many of the centuries old tra-
ditions and practices that have molded Chinese culture.

This is also no doubt the case concerning the PRC's
attitudes toward international law as well as its
treaty practices. Partial bases for many Chinese
practices in international affairs stem from the experience of Imperial China, even predating her contact with the West. As Luke T. Lee so aptly phrases
it,

> It is axiomatic that the present cannot be
> divorced from the past, even in a society cur-
> rently undergoing a "Great Proletarian Cultural
> Revolution." To understand present-day Chinese
> treaty practice one must first grasp the role of
> treaties in traditional China.[32]

It is felt then, that a brief review of the historical background of Chinese international relations
is necessary to establish the proper foundation for
the material to follow.

Until the occurrence of events by which the Chinese Empire was virtually forced into dealing with
the Western nations on the basis of sovereign equality, this concept in international relations was un-
known to the Chinese. Until the time of her dealings with the West, China dealt only with what were
known as her tributary States or dependencies.[33]
The bases for the dealings with these States were
tributes and memorials paid to the Emperor of China
by the subordinate government emissaries. China,
the Middle Kingdom, considered herself unequaled in
the entire world and as standing at the head of the
family of nations comprised of the tributary States
surrounding her borders. China treated the tributary States of Annam, Burma, Korea and Siam by the
superior-inferior role pattern prescribed in Confucian teachings.[34] China became so imbued with this
particular relationship pattern with other States
that in the beginnings of the contacts with the West,
the Imperial Government expected that these new
States should and would conform to this same role
pattern in carrying out their relations with China.

Contact with the West, which subsequently has
been marked consistently by occurrences of violence,
began with the Portuguese in 1511. Portugal was the
first of the Western maritime nations to open direct

relations with the Chinese Empire. They were followed by the Spanish, the Dutch and the English, but none succeeded in doing more than securing "the enrollment of their nation among the tributaries of the Great Emperor, but not to obtain a grant of privileges."[35]

The Treaty of Nertchinsk, signed with Russia in 1689, was China's first treaty with a non-Asian nation. The treaty came about as a result of several skirmishes which had taken place over a number of years involving the demarcation of the boundary between the two countries. It was the first of several agreements effecting a settlement of the Sino-Russian border. A further settlement of the boundary was reached in the Treaty of Kiakhta in 1721.

The Treaty of Nertchinsk, which was negotiated under conditions of Chinese military and naval superiority, was a diplomatic triumph for China. Moreover, it established the conduct of Sino-Russian relations under conditions of Chinese dictates until the mid-1800's.

The Chinese continued to believe that theirs was the empire to which all nations of the world were subservient and continued to dictate the terms by which relations with the Western nations would exist. The situation remained until 1839.

Finally by 1840 pressures brought primarily by

the English, and backed up with demonstrations of
force, began to turn the tide of relations with the
West in the opposite direction. The so called "Opium
War" of the 1840's proved conclusively that the Chinese Empire was no match for the military technology
of the Western powers. As a result of the West's
superior military potential China was forced into
the first of many treaties with the Western powers.
These treaties were subsequently to be known by the
Chinese as "unequal treaties."

The first of these treaties was the Treaty of Nanking, signed on August 29, 1842. It was the first
of four treaties granting concessions to the Western
nations. There could be little doubt of the "unequal"
nature of this treaty. One English author has described this treaty as being,

> ...imposed on China at the mouth of the cannon
> of the British fleet, and under the threat of
> an assault on the city of Nanking by British
> troops.[36]

The Treaty of Nanking in 1842 along with the Treaty of The Bogue in 1843, both with the English, the
Treaty of Wanghia in 1844 with the United States and
the Treaty of Whampoa in 1844 with the French, succeeded in establishing a new framework by which the
West would deal with China. By 1860 it was the West
that was in full control of dictating the conditions

of their common relations.[37]

So general, yet complementary, were the terms of these four treaties, that though they were concluded with three separate Western powers, they could really be treated as constituting a single settlement between Imperial China and the West.

These treaties established clearly, for the first time in a formal document, the equality of the respective governments with the Chinese Empire. In terminology as well as in the manner in which the treaties were written, not only the countries but the heads-of-state were accorded equal status. It was the first time that the Emperor of China had ever been treated as anything but the superior in any document. The plenipotentiaries were also given equal status in the negotiations.[38]

Even more important from China's viewpoint were the infringements on Chinese sovereignty called for in these treaties. The first major infringement on Chinese sovereignty was the establishment of a uniform and moderate tariff known as the "five percent ad valorem treaty tariff." The effect of this provision was that it took from China, for nearly a century, the right to establish her own tariffs.[39]

The second infringement was the provision calling for extra-territorial jurisdiction in criminal cases

established by the Treaty of the Bogue.[40] The pro-
viso of extra-territoriality was further extended
to include civil as well as criminal cases by the
American Treaty of Wanghia (1844). The Western jusi-
fication for the inclusion of extra-territorial jurisdiction in these treaties was an effort to place
their own nationals under a legal system more familiar
to them. There had been several infamous incidents
whereby English and American citizens had been sub-
jected to the Chinese system of justice and the Western powers were unwilling for such incidents to continue.[41] The extra-territorial provisions were, nonetheless, an infringement on Chinese sovereignty.
These provisos ended more or less simultaneously with
the colonial era.[42]

The Treaty of the Bogue also secured for the
English the principle of most-favored-nation treatment. The importance of this concession was not just
in the most-favored-nation principle itself but
rather in the breadth and scope of the provision. It
included virtually any privileges or concessions that
might be granted to any other nation. It should be
noted here that though most-favored-nation clauses
are still a part of Western international law, their
scope is usually limited to specific provisions
such as import duties.[43]

The current use of the most-favored-nation clause
by the People's Republic of China will be discussed
in the following chapter.

These four initial treaties remained the governing
factors in Chinese relations with the West until the
signing of the treaties in Tientsin in 1858. The
signing of these newer treaties, which granted even
further concessions to the West, was brought about by
a short war precipitated by an incident involving the
lorcha Arrow.[44] The war that resulted from the incident was carried out by the British and the French and
again the Chinese found themselves facing superior
military power and found themselves forced into a
treaty virtually at gunpoint. By the end of June,
1858, treaties granting major concessions were signed
with England, France, Russia and the United States.

Russia seized this period of Chinese confrontation
with the West as an opportunity to make territorial
advances on the Northern Chinese border. Although
China had succeeded, in the Treaty of Nertchinsk
(1689), in obtaining the Amur River Valley, they had
made no serious attempts to colonize the area. By
1847 the Tsarist government had established settlements in the Amur Valley well beyond the agreed
boundary of 1689. By August, 1850, Nikolaievsk was

founded at the mouth of the Amur River and by 1853 Sakhalin Island had been annexed. These, along with several other new Russian settlements were well within formerly designated Chinese territory. By this time not only was Russian military strength superior to that of China but the Chinese were still engaged with what appeared to be a more serious threat from the Western nations in the Southern provinces. As a result, during the Arrow war, the Treaty of Aigun was signed with Russia on May 28, 1858. The treaty, negotiated under great duress from the Russians, succeeded in reestablishing the Sino-Russian border at all points demanded by the Tsarist government.[45]

The next landmark treaty to be signed by China was the Treaty of Shimonoseki on April 17, 1895 with Japan. This treaty, like many preceding it, was the product of a war. The Treaty of Shimonoseki was the result of the Sino-Japanese war which ended in 1894. The immediate effects of the treaty were the gaining of concessions by Japan such as to elevate her to the status of a Western power in her dealings with China. Most important of the concessions was the ceding of Formosa (Taiwan), the Pescadores and the Liaotung Peninsula in Southern Manchuria to Japan.

The long term results of the war and the treaty were, however, to be of much greater significance to

China. The Sino-Japanese war and the Treaty of Shimonoseki, with a former member of the Confucian family of nations, one that had gained victory as a result of her Westernization, truly put an end to the
era of Confucian international relations and thrust
China into a world dominated by Western concepts of
treaties and international law.

After the Treaty of Shimonoseki, China was in
great danger of being permanently divided by the
European powers and Japan into colonial possessions.
Several lease arrangements were forced on the Chinese,
giving control of various strategic areas of China
to Russia, Germany and England. Fortunately for China and her continuing existence as a sovereign entity, events in the Western world served to prevent
the final colonization of the Chinese mainland.

The last treaty of major importance entered into
by the Chinese Empire was the Boxer Protocol, signed
on September 7, 1901. The treaty was brought about
as a result of Western intervention in the suppres-
sion of the Boxer Rebellion, an "anti-foreigners"
movement that threatened all holdings of foreign
countries on the mainland of China. England, France,
Germany, Japan, Russia and the United States all provided troops to quell the uprising. These powers
then held the Chinese government responsible, for

what had been a rebel action, and forced it to pay
huge indemnities to them as a result of the war. So
unfair and disproportionate were the indemnities that
substantial portions were returned to China in 1907
and 1924.[46]

The Boxer Protocol also served to aid in the
downfall of the already crumbling Manchu dynasty and
eventually lead to the revolution establishing the
Republic in 1911.

The significance of the history of treaty negotiations by the Republic of China in its short tenure
on the Chinese mainland was its constant struggle to
have returned to China all that had been taken from it
by the West in the preceding 70 years. This period
was also marked by the reluctance of the West to give
up any of the concessions which those nations had
gained from the Manchus. In spite of a new-born
strong Chinese nationalism the Western nations held
fast to what they had.

One of the more notable events, and one which has
had a lasting effect on the PRC's attitudes was the
Treaty of Versailles. China had entered the First
World War on the side of the Allies partly in the hope
of having the German held areas of Shantung returned
to China after the German defeat. But this was not
to be. In spite of an excellent case made by the

Chinese negotiators at the treaty conference, the former German held territory was given over to Japan.
China, as a result, refused to sign the Treaty of Versailles. Chinese Communist writers have many times
since recalled the "betrayal at Versailles" in their
attacks on the capitalist nations.[47]

The Republic of China had attempted, since its
founding, to rid itself of what it considered to be
"unequal" treaties with the West. Little was achieved
however, until after the Kuomintang government of
Chiang Kai-shek was established in June, 1928. The
new government issued a declaration on June 16, 1928
stating that all treaties must be renegotiated on the
basis of sovereignty and equality. It further announced that all expired "unequal" treaties were considered abrogated.[48]

The United States was the first country to negotiate a new treaty conceding tariff autonomy to China.
It was the first time since 1843 that China had the
ability to set her own tariffs without outside inter-
ference.[49] Similar agreements soon followed with the
other powers.

The Republic's efforts to obtain the retroces-
sion of leased territories succeeded only in gaining
the return of Wei-hai-wei from the British. Further
attempts were interrupted by the Japanese invasion

and the subsequent World War.

The foregoing historical review of the foreign relations and treaty negotiations of the Chinese Empire and the Republic of China has, of necessity, been all too brief. It has been more for the purpose of illustration rather than any comprehensive treatment of the subject. Nonetheless, several conclusions may be drawn from the foregoing discussion which should be applicable to an understanding of the PRC's treaty practices.

It is quite evident that all international relations and the resultant treaties between the Chinese Empire and other nations were based on the existing power differentials. China dealt with her tributary states on the basis of the Confucian concept of international relations. She attempted to apply the same set of relationships in her dealings with the West, and for a time, was successful in this venture. The existing power differentials eventually caused the nature of the relationship to shift to one of Western dominance.

The treaties negotiated with China by the other existing powers were all the result of conflict situations and were all completed under vastly unequal power relationships. In many cases the situation could easily have been identified as one of duress against

against the Chinese Empire. So weak was the Empire in
the face of Western military power that it almost suffered colonial partition at the hands of these powers.
The history of relations with the West and other im-
perialistic powers has left a lasting and bitter im-
pression with the Chinese.

China's international relations, since the founding of the Republic in 1911 and continuing through
the People's Republic of today, have been marked by
attempts to reassert China's sovereign independent
status and efforts to recoup the losses of the Empire.
The Republic of China succeeded for the most part in
abrogating all of those treaties which it considered
"unequal." The PRC, however, feels that most of the
treaties negotiated by the Republic were also of an
"unequal" nature and has denounced them as invalid.

Thus there have been three rather distinct
phases in Chinese international relations preceding
the establishment of the People's Republic: one of
Chinese Imperial dominance, one of Western and other
great power dominance brought about by superior tech-
nological and military abilities, and one of rehabili-
tation of Chinese sovereignty and territorial integrity. The People's Republic of China represents
both a continuation of the last phase and a beginning
of a new phase in China's dealings with the world.

[off]

FOOTNOTES

1. Shabtai Rosenne, The Law of Treaties, Dobbs Ferry, New York, 1970, p. 46.

2. Statute of the International Court of Justice, Article 38 (1).

3. Peter H. Rohn, "Institutionalism in the Law of Treaties: A Case of Combining Teaching and Research," American Society of International Law Proceedings, 1965, pp. 93-98.

4. The United Nations Charter, Article 102 (1).

5. Rosenne, op. cit., p. 47.

6. For a thorough discussion of this particular phenomenon using recently established Asian States as examples see J.J.G. Syatauw, Some Newly Established Asian States and the Development of International Law, The Hague, Martinus Nijhoff, 1961.

7. Vienna Convention on the Law of Treaties, 1969, Section 4, Article 34.

8. F.I. Kozhevnikov, ed., International Law, Moscow, Foreign Languages Publishing House, n.d., p. 247.

9. See for example, Georg Schwarzenberger, A Manual of International Law, New York, Praeger, 1967, pp. 11-15.

10. There have been several compilations made of the treaties of the PRC and because different criteria were used for the inclusion of the documents in the study no agreed upon number of treaties exists. It is therefore difficult to get an absolute ranking. Using the 1,660 treaties included in the present study in comparison with the UNTS data the PRC ranks third in the world.

11. It is realized that all may not be in complete agreement with such a statement. Holsti and Sullivan have mentioned the problem in their study in the following manner: "The importance of such data as indicators of Chinese foreign policy is not universally accepted. Karl Wittfogel, for example, asserts that, 'In the course of this intricate process the leading Communist countries may have grave dif-

ferences of opinion on details of economic cooperation
and domestic foreign policy. But any analyst who, because of such secondary differences, disregards the
primary ties between Moscow and Peking, appraises the
Communist power system with the standards of a Babbitt
or a Colonel Blimp.' Wittfogel, 'A Stronger Oriental
Despotism,' The China Quarterly, No. 1, (January-
March, 1960), 34. At the risk of being guilty of bab-
bitry, we assume that our data do in fact shed some
light on the current state of Sino-Soviet relations."
Ole R. Holsti and John D. Sullivan, "National-International Linkages: France and China as Nonconforming
Alliance Members," James Rosenau, ed., Linkage Politics, New York, The Free Press, 1969, pp. 147-195.

12. See remark by Aleksandr Troianovskii quoted
in Jan F. Triska and Robert M. Slusser, The Theory,
Law and Policy of Soviet Treaties, Stanford, Stanford
University Press, 1962, p. 9; also see Douglas John-
ston, "Chinese Treaty Policy and Practices: A Multi-
Method Scheme of Analysis," paper presented to the
American Society of International Law, New York City,
New School of Social Research, February 7-8, 1969.

13. Other quantitative treaty studies include:
L. Jerold Adams, Theory, Law and Policy of Contempo-
rary Japanese Treaties, Dobbs Ferry, New York, Oceana,
1974. L. Jerold Adams, "Japanese Treaty Patterns,"
Asian Survey, Vol. 12, No. 3 (March 1972) pp. 242-258;
Juris A. Lejnieks, "The Nomenclature of Treaties: A
Quantitative Analysis," The Texas International Law
Forum, Vol. II, No. 2, pp. 175-188; Peter H. Rohn, The
Turkish Treaties in Global Perspective," The Turkish
Yearbook of International Law, 1965, pp. 119-160; Pe-
ter H. Rohn, "Canada in the United Nations Treaty Se-
ries: A Global Perspective," The Canadian Yearbook of
International Law, 1966, pp. 102-130; Gary L. Scott,
"Treaties of the People's Republic of China: A Quan-
titative Analysis," Asian Survey, Vol. 13, No. 5, (May,
1973), pp. 496-512; Jan F. Triska, "Soviet Treaty Law:
A Quantitative Analysis," Law and Contemporary Prob-
lems, Vol. 29, No. 3, pp. 866-909; William M. Vaughn,
"Finding the Law of Expropriation: Traditional v.
Quantitative Research," The Texas International Law
Forum, Vol. II, No. 2, pp. 189-205. Most of the above
cited publications were prepared under the auspices of
the Treaty Information Project, University of Washington, Seattle, Washington, Peter H. Rohn, Director.
For a general description of the project see Peter
H. Rohn, "The United Nations Treaty Series Project,"
International Studies Quarterly, Vol. 12, No. 2 (June
1968) pp. 174-195.

14. Chung-hua jen-min kung-ho-kuo t'iao-yueh-
chi, (Compilation of Treaties of the People's Republic of China, 1949-64) (TYC).

15. Douglas M. Johnston and Hungdah Chiu, eds.,
Agreements of the People's Republic of China, 1949-
1967: A Calendar, Cambridge, Harvard University Press,
1968. Other sources used in this study include,
Peking Review; Jen-min jih-pao (People's Daily;
Peking); Survey China Mainland Press, U.S. Consulate,
Hong Kong. This type of subjective selection of PRC
treaties for purposes of analysis is not without pre-
cedent. See for example, Luke T. Lee, China and International Agreements, Durham, N.C., Rule of Law
Press, 1969, pp. 18-22.

16. Though contracts are not normally included
in the study of a State's international agreements,
they are included here due to the Chinese reliance
on them to conclude international arrangements that
would usually be concluded by other countries in the
form of protocols and exchanges of notes. Due to
the State ownership of business in China, these contracts especially when concluded with other Socialist
States, have a definite international legal character
and it is felt that their inclusion does not distort
the data base.

17. As no official written criteria exist, only
the author's familiarization with the United Nations
Treaty Series has served as a guide for establishing
the criteria. The author has worked for one year as
a research assistant on the on-going Treaty information Project at the University of Washington. See
Rohn, supra, note 13.

18. This type of information is given in the
UNTS as annex information and is not given a separate
treaty number but rather is listed under the number
of the original agreement.

19. See Johnston and Chiu, op. cit., p. viii.

20. Ibid.

21. TYC, 1949-64, op. cit.

22. James C. Hsiung, Law and Policy in China's
Foreign Relations, New York, Columbia University
Press, 1972, p. 250.

32

23.   Rohn, Canadian Yearbook, op. cit.

24.   U.N. Charter, Article 102(1).

25.   Rohn, Turkish Yearbook, op. cit.; and Rohn, Canadian Yearbook, op. cit.; For comparisons with some other countries, including the Soviet Union, see above-cited case study of Canada, p. 20, Table 1 by John H. Kress and Robert V. Edington.

26.   Ingunn Means, Norway Treaty Series Gap Study, unpublished seminar paper, University of Washington, Winter, 1969.

27.   Rohn, supra, note 13.

28.   Rosenne, op. cit.

29.   Triska and Slusser, op. cit.

30.   Among the more recent works on the subject of China, international law and treaties are: Hungdah Chiu, The People's Republic of China and the Law of Treaties, Cambridge, Harvard University Press, 1972. Jerome A. Cohen, ed., Chinese Practice of International Law: Some Case Studies, Cambridge, Harvard University Press, 1973; Cohen, The Dynamics of China's Foreign Relations, Harvard Asian Monograph #39, Cambridge, Harvard University Press, 1970; Jerome A. Cohen and Hungdah Chiu, People's China and International Law: A Documentary Study, Princeton, New Jersey, Princeton University Press, 1974; James C. Hsiung, op. cit.; Luke T. Lee, op. cit.; Leng Shao-chuan and Hungdah Chiu, Law in Chinese Foreign Policy: Communist China: and Selected Problems of International Law, Dobbs Ferry, New York, Oceana, 1972.

31.   Cohen and Chiu, op. cit., p. xiii.

32.   Lee, op. cit.

33.   The name of the agency for handling relations with foreign States prior to contact with the West gives some clue to the attitude of China toward other States.   The agency was designated Hui-t'ung ssu-ku kuan (Residence for Envoys of the Four Tributary States).

34.   Confucius, The Great Learning, Ch. 1, (E. Pound translation, 1939) cited in Lee, op. cit., p.25.

33

35. Hosea B. Morse, The International Relations of the Chinese Empire, Vol. I, London, Longmans, Green and Co., 1910, p. 49.

36. Ibid., p. 298

37. Texts of these four agreements and other important nineteenth century Chinese treaties are contained in Treaties, Conventions, etc., Between China and Foreign States, 2 Vols., 2nd ed., Shanghai, 1917.

38. Morse, op. cit.

39. For a discussion of China's tariff problem see, S.F. Wright, China's Struggle for Tariff Autonomy, Shanghai, Kelly Walsh Ltd., 1938.

40. For text of Article IX, Treaty of Humen Chai, signed at the Bogue, October 8, 1843 and other most-favored-nation clauses see supra, note 36.

41. Among such incidents were the execution by strangulation of an English sailor from the ship Lady Hughes on January 8, 1785 and the execution of the American sailor Terranova, from the ship Emily. Both were put to death for causing the death of a Chinese.

42. Schwarzenberger, op. cit., pp. 8, 170.

43. See for example, Whitney v Robertson, Supreme Court of the United States, 1888. 124 U.S. 190, 8S Ct. 456, 31L. Ed. 386, cited in Friedmann, Lissitzyn and Pugh, International Law: Cases and Materials, St. Paul, Minn., West, 1969, pp. 364-365.

44. For a detailed account of the affair of the lorcha Arrow and the subsequent war see, Paul H. Clyde, The Far East: A History of the Impact of the West on Eastern Asia, New York, Prentice Hall, 1948, pp. 150-159; and Morse, op. cit., pp. 422-427.

45. Clyde, op. cit., p. 167.

46. The total indemnity demanded from China was $333 million. The American share of the indemnity was $25 million. For other details of the settlement see Clyde, op. cit., pp. 300-302.

47. Hsiung, op. cit., p. 87.

48. The China Yearbook 1929-1930, p. 824.

49. The text of the MacMurray-Soong Treaty appears in Foreign Relations, Vol. II, 1928, pp. 449-491. Also see Wright, op. cit., pp. 633-634.

CHAPTER II

CHINESE ATTITUDES AND PRACTICES
IN INTERNATIONAL LAW

The Role of Treaties in PRC Practice

It has been demonstrated that treaties play a
major role as source and substance of Western international law. It would seem, then, that to study
the treaty practices of any nation subscribing to the
principles of that body of law would be a useful un-
dertaking; one that would indeed add a significant dimension to the predictability of that nation's behavior in the international system. If, however, the
analysis should focus on a nation which does not have
the same regard for the obligations that are created
by treaties as do the majority of nations in the international system, then the validity of our indicator
may be suspect.

If we are to rely on data derived from a quantitative analysis of Chinese treaties we must be reasonably assured that treaties specifically and international legal obligations in general are of serious
concern to the People's Republic of China. For if
it can be shown that China has little regard for international law and treaty commitments, then it can
reasonably be asserted that there is little point in

35

studying these relatively meaningless documents as
an indicator of Chinese behavior.

The People's Republic of China has, in the past,
been severely criticized for its recalcitrant behavior as a subject of international law. One author
in commenting on the PRC's early international dealings has suggested that it did not even bother to pay
lip service to international law. He further noted
that their revolutionary ethic was, "thoroughly in-
compatible with the existing structure of international law and relations."[1]

In 1963 the United States Department of State
published a document in which it charged the PRC
with numerous violations of treaties and international
law.[2] The charges include alleged PRC violation of
the Korean Armistice Agreement of 1953, violation of
the trade agreements between India and the PRC signed
on April 29, 1953 and October 14, 1954, and violation
of the 1955 Agreed Measures Announcement between the
United States and the PRC regarding the repatriation
of civilians.[3] In most of the above cited cases the
United States charged the PRC with numerous violations
of each agreement.

Nor do the charges against the PRC all derive
from American sources. India and the Soviet Union,
among others, have repeatedly charged that China has

violated various treaties and other rules of international law.[4]

It is difficult to make an accurate assessment
of the validity of the various allegations. The vagaries of treaty interpretations are known to all who
study the international legal system.[5] In the case
of the PRC and its dealings with States accustomed to
the Western practice of international law it is not
difficult to see that the vagaries of treaty interpretation may be manifoldly exacerbated by differences in culture, ideology, legal precepts and general Weltanschauung of the relative States.

Though it is not within the scope of this study
to examine the nature of each alleged violation by
the PRC of its treaty commitments, it will, nonetheless, be helpful to investigate one of the more notable cases by way of example.

Among the violations charged by the United States
is the failure of the PRC to live up to the terms of
the Agreed Measures Announcement of September 10,
1955. In spite of doubts arising over the legal character of the announcement, each side holds the other
responsible for failure of the announcement to achieve
its intended purpose of insuring the rapid repatriation of civilians held in the United States and
China.[6]

In view of the political situation at the time
and the refusal of the United States to recognize
the PRC the intended agreement took the awkward form
of simultaneous but separate "announcements" by each
side. The "agreement" was for the intended purpose
of exchanging American and Chinese civilians, and
was worded (possibly intentionally) in an extremely
vague manner. Both governments agreed to adopt
"appropriate measures" so that civilians from their
respective countries might "expeditiously exercise
their right to return."[7]

Disputes arose during the implementation stage
over whether or not American prisoners in China
were to be included under the general term "civilians."[8] The United States also became disturbed over
the slowness with which the Chinese were releasing
people for repatriation. A 1969 report by the Subcommittee on National Security and International
Operations exemplifies the United States' position
on the agreement.

> Washington and Peking concluded an agreement
> in six hard weeks of negotiations. This sin-
> gle agreement (the only concluded transaction
> that the U.S. has had on a government to gov-
> ernment basis with Peking) was promptly vio-
> lated by Peking, from the American standpoint
> and became a matter of bitter dispute between
> the two countries. Peking did not immediately
> release the American prisoners as the Ameri-
> cans sincerely thought the agreement meant and
> the prisoners were dribbled out of China over

a long period of time. As of 1969 a few Ameri-
cans were still in Chinese jails.[9]

The PRC was equally disgruntled by what it per-
ceived to be U.S. violations of the agreement. The
Chinese claimed that in spite of U.S. insistence that
prisoners should be included under the generic term
"civilians", Chinese prisoners in the United States
had not been released long after students and scien-
tists had been repatriated.[10] Claims and counter
claims continued the dissatisfaction on both sides.
So great was the PRC dissatisfaction with the agreement that in 1960 when the U.S. presented a similar
agreement to the Chinese ambassador at Warsaw, concerning an exchange of correspondents, he refused
it on the grounds that,

> We remember that the agreement of the two
> sides on the return of civilians to their
> countries also took this form. But the fact
> that the United States' side has so far
> failed to seriously implement the agreement
> shows that this form does not have enough
> binding force on the U.S. side. To prevent
> the U.S. side from again violating the agree-
> ment the Chinese side resolutely maintains
> that all agreements between the two sides
> must take the form of joint announcements
> of both sides and no longer take that of [11]
> statements issued by the two sides separately.

Most of the disagreements that arose over the
Agreed Measures Announcement were a result of different interpretations of the wording. For example,
the term "civilians" was not defined, and while the

U.S. thought it included prisoners, the PRC did not.
At a later date the U.S. State Department admitted
that during the 14 sessions of Ambassadorial Talks,
from which the agreement arose, no mention was made
of "prisoners" specifically on either side.[12]

J.C. Hsiung has characterized the dispute in
the following manner:

> The whole controversy, viewed from hind-
> sight and with the detachment afforded by the
> lapse of a decade and a half, may perhaps be
> better characterized as one growing out of
> mutual suspicion and distrust, with attendant
> difficulties in the interpretation of the
> specific provisions of the agreement reached
> by the two adversaries. As such it is a case
> falling more under conflicts arising from
> treaty interpretation than outright treaty
> violations.[13]

Hsiung and Luke T. Lee have discussed many of
the other alleged treaty violations by the PRC and
have arrived at similar conclusions concerning them.[14]

In the following discussion I shall attempt to
show that Communist China's attitude toward international law, though differing in some respects from
the traditional Western viewpoint is, nonetheless,
serious and intended to contribute to a viable system
of inter-state relations and world order. In doing
so it is hoped that the treaties of the People's
Republic of China will emerge as an equally reliable
source for analysis and comparison as those treaties
of nations subscribing wholly to the tenets of West-

ern international law.

In order to fully comprehend the PRC's views of international law it will be necessary to approach the problem on several levels.

The most basic level and the one that will be discussed first is the Chinese view of the nature of law in general, i.e. including both municipal and international law.

The Chinese Concept of Law

It has been traditional for Western legal scholars, at least since the democratic revolution of the 17th and 18th centuries, to view law as a fixed set of rules deriving somehow from the people and held binding on them. This view is central to the proposition that the individual is the most important factor in society and that the needs and desires of the group and the State are of secondary importance. Moreover, in the Western system of law there is a strongly felt need for codified law with the express purpose of eliminating, in so far as possible, arbitrariness by the rulers which might tend to mitigate the intended purpose of the law.

Although there are some Western scholars who view law as an instrument for social change, in the Western legal system it is more often than not the

case that law is seen as reflecting rather than causing societal change. Thus we have, in theory at
least, a set of semi-static laws which govern the
actions of society by a system known, not altogether
correctly, as "the Rule of Law."

The Chinese, on the other hand, have long
viewed law in a very different way. Their concept
of law is based on a system of norms under which the
group and the State are regarded as being the primary
entities to be served. The individual is of secondary importance and his full worth can only be a-
chieved in service to the larger collective entity.

The PRC view of law combines the traditional
Chinese legal precepts as exemplified in the concepts of li and fa[15] with the more modern concepts
drawn from Marxism-Leninism. It arrives at a view
of law that closely resembles that of the Soviet
Union, particularly through the 1950's.

The Chinese Communist view of law in general
combines legal principles derived from all phases
of China's long cultural heritage. From Confucian
times comes the principle of governing in accordance with approved social norms (li). This is combined with governing in accordance with positive
law (fa), derived from the ancient Chinese Legalist
school. The law of li assures proper behavior

through moral example and gentle persuasion whereas the law of _fa_ depends on coercion and deterrence to achieve compliance.

The Chinese Communists have relied heavily on both of these methods and principles of law. Much of the ideological doctrine and social pressures are aimed at assuring compliance through the principle of overriding social norms, (li). However, they have, nonetheless, maintained a rather rigorous system of criminal sanctions.[16]

In addition to principles gained from ancient Chinese law, China, since 1928, has consciously borrowed from legal systems outside of the traditional Chinese legal model to establish a legal system more in line with the contemporary nation-state. Chiang Kai-shek's nationalist party (Kuomintang) borrowed from the Western system of law in order to perfect codes of criminal law and procedure similar to those of continental Europe.[17] The Chinese Communists, on the other hand, even from their earliest beginnings in the late 1920's and 1930's, sought to borrow legal institutions and practices from the Soviet Union. The Soviet Union had, of course, also borrowed heavily from, and been passively influenced by, Western European systems of law. One thing, however, that was not assimilated into the Soviet, the Nation-

alist Chinese or the Communist Chinese systems of law
was the syndrome of values and attitudes that were the
major underpinnings of the Western system of law and
government. In practice both of the Chinese governments as well as the Soviet Union have little concern
for such issues as human rights or the safeguards of
the accused. Consistently throughout China's history
it was the State and not the individual for whose
benefit the laws were drawn. As Jerome Cohen points
out,

> When one compares the uses of law in
> traditional China, in the Republic of China
> (located on Taiwan since 1949), and in the
> People's Republic of China, significant
> differences of course appear. Yet one ma-
> jor similarity stands out - law and legal
> institutions still serve principally as in-
> struments for enhancing the power of the
> States and for disciplining the people to
> carry out its policies. In the Chinese
> value system the interests of the state
> and the group have always dwarfed those of
> the individual.[18]

In addition to these differences which exist
between China and the West regarding law, there is
another crucial and fundamental distinction that bears
directly on the Chinese practice of international law.
In the West, law, in so far as possible, is seen to
be necessarily divorced from politics. In the PRC
this view would be branded as "rightist heresy."[19]

This particular view of law is exemplified in
a statement made by Shen Chu-ju, the first President

of the Supreme People's Court. Shen stated,

> Our judicial work must serve political
> ends actively and must be brought to
> bear on current political tasks and the
> mass movement.[20]

This concept of law as the political instrument of the
State carries over to international law in PRC theory
as it does in Soviet theory.

The PRC and International Law

The Chinese attitude toward the nature of international law specifically can best be exemplified in
a passage from Chou Fu-lun's oft cited article, "An
Inquiry into the Nature of Modern International Law."

> International law, in addition to
> being a body of principles and norms
> which must be observed by every country,
> is also, just as any law, a political
> instrument; whether a country is social-
> ist or capitalist, it will to a certain
> degree utilize international law in im-
> plementing its foreign policy.[21]

This particular view coincides quite closely with
one found in a Soviet text on international law which
defines international law as,

> ... the aggregate of rules governing rela-
> tions between States in the process of
> their conflict and co-operation, designed
> to safeguard their peaceful coexistence,
> expressing the will of the ruling classes
> of these States and defended in case of
> need by coercion applied by States indi-
> vidually or collectively.[22]

The definitional statements above, of course, do
not reflect the totality of opinion on international

law by scholars in either the People's Republic of China or the Soviet Union.

A misperception often exists about so-called totalitarian regimes that there can be only one opinion or statement, coinciding with the party line, regarding such an important subject as international law. That is only slightly less false, however, in these countries than in such countries as the United States where we find various scholars writing different opinions as to what the nature, substance and purpose of international law is and should be.[23]

For example, we can see that at least one writer, Chu Li-lu, takes a much more radical approach to international law than does his contemporary Chou Fu-lun. Chu goes so far as to state that if international law is

> useful to our country, to Socialist enterprise, or to the peace enterprise of the world, we will use it. However, if this instrument is disadvantageous to our country, to Socialist enterprises or to peace enterprises of the people of the world, we will not use it and should create a new instrument to replace it.[24]

Definitional and attitudinal statements toward international law in general, while helpful, nonetheless do not go far enough. It is necessary therefore, to discuss the attitudes of the PRC toward certain specific critical segments of international

law, particularly those segments which bear most
closely on the subject at hand, that is treaty practices. As treaty law specifically will be dealt with
in depth in the following Chapter, this discussion
will be concerned briefly with a few issues of international law which relate to the overall issue.

Sovereignty

The Chinese Communist view of sovereignty resembles very closely the Soviet doctrine of illimitable sovereignty held in the initial years of the
Soviet Union. This is generally to be expected of
any developing nation and it can probably be assumed
that the PRC, like the Soviet Union, as it achieves
a more stable position in the hierarchy of world order, will also mitigate its stand toward illimitable
sovereignty. The current Soviet view, for example,
as expressed in a 1961 Soviet text on international
law, shows considerable change from the original concept of illimitable sovereignty.

> The definitive importance of the prin-
> ciple of sovereignty in relations between
> States is not the same thing as the con-
> ception of "absolute" sovereignty. A so-
> vereign State must not in its international
> relations behave in an arbitrary fashion,
> without taking account of the generally re-
> cognized principles of International Law
> and the international undertakings which it
> has voluntarily assumed. To do so would
> mean to violate the principle of sovereign
> equality of all the members of the interna-

tional community. It would undermine the
international community and lead to the un-
limited rule of force and violence.[25]

The Chinese doctrine of illimitable sovereignty,
in its as yet unmitigated form, is probably a result
of the combination of three factors. Those factors
in probable order of importance are, (1) a new found
ideologically based nationalism, (2) China's own historical experiences in dealing with the West and (3)
Soviet influences. China, like many of the newly
emerging nations of the world, has had some bitter
historical experiences in dealing with the Western
nations of the world. One can be relatively certain
that events and policies such as the Opium War, The
Open Door Policy, the United States and British
warships' bombardment of Nanking in 1927, the establishment of puppet regimes, the capitulatory or
extraterritorial jurisdiction, and the practice of
"concessions" are still vivid memories to the Chinese.
In light of these past experiences it is not surprising that the Chinese Communists are so jealous of
their new found State sovereignty. Unlike any other
period in Chinese history since the "opening of China," China is at last able to defend her territorial
integrity and legal sovereignty. With this new
found ability it is not surprising that she is unwilling to compromise her State sovereignty for any

kind of Western considerations. Sovereignty is viewed by the PRC as the core of all fundamental principles of international law and furthermore, as the legal foundation on which its institutions and norms are based.[26]

There are three major elements in the Chinese Communist doctrine of sovereignty. First, the infringement of PRC sovereignty shall not be tolerated. Second, the PRC is committed to respecting the sovereignty of other states. Third, the PRC will never surrender her own sovereign interests or "sell out" these interests of other States to the imperialists.[27]

Thus the PRC is not only a strict defender of her own sovereignty but intends to sell herself to the world as the defender of the sovereignty of all other States unable to do so on their own.

The PRC attitude and doctrine of State sovereignty do not always correspond to her practice in international affairs. It hardly need be pointed out that the entering into treaties and other agreements with other States, and more recently, participation in a global body such as the United Nations, is in itself a de facto limitation of State sovereignty. However, in other areas, such as dispute settlement, there is great similarity between the PRC's actual

practice and the doctrine of State sovereignty. The
PRC is, for example, reluctant to have any disputes
settled by third party intervention. It also disavows the use of any third party judicial body such
as the International Court of Justice. It disavows
the use of such a body on the basis that it is a violation of State sovereignty and that it has, like the
United Nations, "degenerated into a tool of American
Imperialism."[28]

Sources of International Law

The sources of international law subscribed to
by Western States are listed in Article 38 of the
Statute of the International Court of Justice. They
include in order of importance, international conventions (treaties), international custom, general principles of international law recognized by civilized
nations, judicial decisions and the writings of leading publicists.

The PRC is not in full agreement with this particular list of the sources of international law.
Marxist-Leninist doctrine has, to a large extent, influenced PRC writers in their attitudes towards the
sources of international law. An example of the influence of this doctrine can be seen in the writings of Ying T'ao. Concerning the sources of international law, he writes, "the substantive sources of

bourgeois international law are the external policy
of the bourgeoisie which is also the will of the
ruling class of those big capitalist powers."[29]   He
further sees that the emphasis by Western nations on
"formal" sources of international law is a deception
created to deceive the people into thinking that international law does not possess class character.[30]
The PRC also condemns the usage of the phrase "law
recognized by civilized nations," as exhibiting the
class character of international law.

As to what the PRC considers as formal sources
of international law is unclear. A Chinese book of
selected documents on international law lists most
of the sources subscribed to by Western nations under
the heading "sources of international law." It is
not clear however, to which of these, if any, the PRC
subscribes since the book has been produced "for
reference only."[31]

It seems reasonably clear from practice that the
PRC does regard treaties and custom as important
sources of international law. The degree to which
they rely on treaties will be discussed in the following chapter. The PRC is frequently calling on
international custom to defend its stand on many matters. It often considers that many principles em-
bodied in such documents as the United Nations Charter

merely restate what the PRC has long advocated as part of international custom.

The PRC rarely invokes judicial decisions as indicators of international law and, as noted above, they do not believe in third party judicial decisions. They have, however, used the ICJ ruling on the 1951 Anglo-Norwegian Fisheries Case to justify their position on the adoption of the straight-base-line method of determining their territorial waters.

The PRC opinion on the writings of leading publicists is also unclear. They often denounce Western writers but also often use their opinions to support their own position on various matters.

If any conclusions can be drawn concerning the PRC views of the sources of international law they are that: (1) the theoretical base for a fully articulated theory concerning this aspect of international law has not been formulated and (2) their view of the sources of international law at this point is based primarily on political considerations and is goal achievement oriented. As the PRC develops further and undergoes what might be called a maturation process as an international actor, there seems little doubt that their views will become less mercurial and idiosyncratic and come closer to resembling Western standards in this matter.

The Five Principles of Peaceful Coexistence

According to the PRC one of the most important concepts to be included in treaties, and upon which all State relations should be governed, are the Five Principles of Peaceful Coexistence. The Five Principles (wu-hsiang yuan-tse) commonly known to most Western scholars by their Indian name Panch Shila, were first enunciated by Jawaharlal Nehru on June 28, 1954. They were then reaffirmed by Chou En-lai in a joint communique issued with Prime Minister U Nu of Burma the following day.[33] The Five Principles include the following:

(1) Mutual respect for each other's territorial integrity and sovereignty;

(2) Mutual non-aggression;

(3) Mutual non-interference in each other's internal affairs;

(4) Equality and mutual benefit;

(5) Peaceful coexistence.

Several things should be noted about the Five Principles. First, they do not represent any significant departure from any of the overriding principles or jus cogens of Western international law in spite of the fact that in the initial stages of their use they appear to have been hailed by the PRC as new and progressive norms and even as lex ferenda.[34]

However, as early as 1955, one writer in the PRC,
Chou Keng-sheng, attempted to find the basis of the
Five Principles in the fundamental principles of law
accepted by all States.[35]

Second, though the Chinese take credit for the
creation of the Five Principles, Nehru's role in that
venture is not to be overlooked. There is, however,
some basis for the PRC claim to have created the
Five Principles since they appear to be an expansion
of the three principles enunciated in the 1949 Common
Program and later expanded in the Preamble to the
Constitution of the People's Republic of China
adopted on September 20, 1954 by the First National
People's Congress of The People's Republic of China
at its first session.[36]

Finally, the Five Principles have been incorporated in many of the PRC's treaties since 1954. The
Five Principles were first incorporated in a treaty
in the preamble to the Agreement between the People's
Republic of China and India on Trade and Intercourse
between India and Tibet on April 29, 1954.[37] The
Five Principles have been included in 10 Friendship
Treaties through 1965.[38] In addition, the Five Principles or references to them have been included in
many other official and semi-official agreements and
communiques.[39] The inclusion of the Five Principles

is usually reserved for treaties between the PRC and those nations which it considers to be sympathetic with its principles.

The Five Principles of Peaceful Coexistence are of great theoretical importance to the People's Republic of China. Their insistence that they be included in treaties with those nations sympathetic to their political outlook is further evidence of the importance that the PRC attaches to treaties in the governance of their international affairs.

In summary then, the PRC concedes treaties a high place among the sources of international law, though it is difficult to assess from PRC writers whether they occupy the primary place. In general the PRC seems to follow carefully most of the concepts set forth in Western international law, though they are more often than not politically motivated in their application of the law.

In so far as treaty compliance is concerned, most of the difficulties that the PRC has experienced have been over the matter of treaty interpretation and not outright violations of certain agreements. In general the treaties of the PRC should serve as an accurate measure of their international behavior and a predictor of their intentions in the international system.

FOOTNOTES

1. H. Arthur Steiner, "The Mainsprings of Chiese Communist Foreign Policy," American Journal of International Law, Vol. 54 No. 1 (January, 1950); cited in James C. Hsiung, Law and Policy in China's Foreign Relations, New York, Columbia University Press, 1972, pp. 4-5.

2. Department of State, The Conduct of Communist China, Washington D.C., U.S. Government Printing Office, 1963. Prepared for the House Committee on Foreign Affairs, 88th Congress, 1st Session. See esp. pp. 8-9.

3. For an analysis of these allegations see Hsiung, supra note 1, pp. 276-284.

4. Hsiung, op. cit.

5. For a thorough discussion of the problem of treaty interpretation and some possible solutions thereof see, Myres S. McDougal, Harold D. Laswell and James C. Miller, The Interpretation of Agreements and World Public Order, New Haven, Yale University Press, 1967.

6. For a discussion of the legal character of the Announcement see Infra Ch. III, pp. 54-56.

7. TYC 4:1; English text of the announcement appears in Kenneth Young, Negotiating with the Chinese Communists: The United States Experience, 1953-1967, New York, McGraw Hill, 1968, pp. 412-413; Also see "U. S., Red China Announce Measures for Return of Civilians," Department of State Bulletin, no. 847 (Sept. 19, 1955).

8. Hsiung, op. cit., p. 276.

9. Subcommittee for National Security and International Operations, Problems of Negotiation with Communist China, Washington D.C., February, 1969.

10. Hsiung, op. cit., p. 278

11. Quoted in Hungdah Chiu, "Certain Legal Aspects of Communist China's Treaty Practice," Proceedings, American Society of International Law, April, 1967, p. 120.

57

12. New York Times, January 30, 1967; Also see Hsiung, op. cit., p. 278.

13. Hsiung, op. cit., p. 279.

14. Luke T. Lee, China and International Agreements, Durham, N.C., Rule of Law Press, 1969, passim; and Hsiung, pp. 276-284.

15. Lee, op. cit., pp. 133-163.

16. Jerome Alan Cohen, The Criminal Process in the People's Republic of China, 1949-1963, Cambridge, Harvard University Press, 1968, p. 5.

17. Cohen, op. cit., p. 7.

18. Ibid.

19. Hungdah Chiu, "International Law and a Universal System," in Shao-Chuan Leng and Hungdah Chiu, eds., Law in Chinese Foreign Policy: Communist China and Selected Problems of International Law, Dobbs Ferry, New York, Oceana, 1972, p. 2.

20. "Report on Judicial Work to the First National Committee of the Chinese People's Political Consultative Conference," JMJP, October 30, 1951; cited in Chiu, supra note 19.

21. Chou Fu-lun, "An Inquiry into the Nature of Modern International Law," Chiao-hsueh yu yen-chiu (Teaching and Research), No. 3, 1958 pp. 52-56.

22. F.I. Kozhevnikov, ed., International Law, Moscow, Foreign Languages Publishing House, n.d., p. 7.

23. See for example Richard Falk's discussion of "Alwyn V. Freeman v. Myres S. McDougal," American Journal of International Law, V. 59, no.1 (January 1965), p. 66.

24. Chiu, supra, note 19, p. 3.

25. Kozhevnikov, ed., op. cit., pp. 96-97.

26. Hsiung, op. cit., pp. 72-73.

27. Ibid.

28. "International Court of Justice--A Shelter

for Gangsters," JMJP (July 29, 1966), p. 6, quoted in
Jerome A. Cohen and Hungdah Chiu, People's China and
International Law: A Documentary Study, Princeton,
Princeton University Press, 1974, p. 1444; see also
Hsiung, op. cit., p. 201.

29.   Ying T'ao, "Recognize the True Face of Bour-
geois International Law from a few Basic Concepts,"
Kuo-chi wen-t'i yen-chiu, (Studies in International
Problems), No. 1, Peking, 1960, pp. 46-47.

30.   Ibid.

31.   Chiu, supra, note 19, p. 10.

32.   Tao Cheng, "The Law of the Sea," in Leng
and Chiu, esp., op. cit., pp. 79-114.

33.   The English text of the communique may be
found in G.V. Ambekar and V.D. Divekar, eds., Documents on China's Relations with South and Southeast
Asia (1949-1962), Bombay,Allied Publishers, 1964.,
pp. 7-9; cited in James C. Hsiung, "Peaceful Coexistence and Its Correlation with Proletarian Interna-
tionalism," in Leng and Chiu, eds., op. cit., p. 36.

34.   See for example, Mao To, "The Important
Achievements of the Conference of Afro-Asian Jurists,"
Cheng-fa yen chiu, (Studies in Politics and Law) no. 2,
1958, pp. 3-9.

35.   Chou Keng-sheng, "The Principle of Peaceful
Coexistence from the Viewpoint of International Law,"
Cheng-fa yen-chiu, (Studies in Politics and Law) No. 6,
1955, pp. 37-41; For an analysis of Professor Chou's
treatise see Hsiung, supra, note 1, pp. 37-47.

36.   Constitution of the People's Republic of
China, Peking, Foreign Language Press, pp. 5-6.

37.   TYC 3:1, UNTS 299:70.

38.   Chiu, supra, note 19, p. 4.

39.   Ibid.

CHAPTER III

TREATY LAW AND THE PRC

The Role of Treaties in PRC Theory and Practice

The exact place of treaties in international law is not so clearly defined for the PRC as it is for either the Soviet Union or for States subscribing wholly to the principles of Western international law. In both of the latter cases it is clear from definitive statements as well as practice that treaties occupy the principal place among sources of international law. In regard to the PRC however, the evidence must be pieced together in order to make some reasonable assumptions, and, as is especially important in the case of the PRC, doctrine must be balanced against practice.

The position taken by PRC legal scholars on the role of treaties in international law seems at first to be similar to that expressed by the Soviet Union. The Soviet Union's position is that treaties are the most important source of international law.[1] While there seems to be no writer in the PRC willing to state the point quite so strongly as the Soviets, it is nonetheless clear that the PRC does regard treaties as one of the important sources of international law. One PRC writer, Wei Liang, states that "treaties

59

are an important source of international law and an
important form of expressing international law."[2]
Another writer, Wang Yao-t'ien, suggests the importance of treaties in governing relations in such an
ideologically diverse world. For since treaties create legally binding norms and obligations they are
indispensable in assuring stable international relations between ideologically divergent nations.[3] However, it should also be noted that the PRC considers
only "equal treaties" as sources of international law
and has been critical of Western nations for failing
to appreciate the differences between just and unjust
obligations created by treaties. In other words, according to Ying T'ao, the important thing is to consider the substance of the treaty in determining if it
is appropriate to classify it as one contributing to
international law and as a source thereof.

> Since bourgeois scholars state that treaties
> are the principal source of international
> law, may we ask where those treaties come
> from? By referring to the large number
> of treaties concluded in the period of
> capitalism, it may be proved that these
> treaties were all concluded under the
> guidance of the external policy of capital-
> ist countries, in accordance with the de-
> mand of the bourgeoisie and through dip-
> lomatic means and arbitrary external prac-
> tices.[4]

The sheer volume of PRC treaties alone is enough
to indicate that the PRC considers treaties as an
extremely important factor in regulating international
intercourse. Since 1949 the PRC has concluded well
over 2,000 international agreements. The 1660 treaties selected for this study represent only the more
formal types of agreements as included in the United
Nations Treaty Series. These documents alone rank
the PRC as one of the world's leading treaty makers.
A country that relies to this extent on treaties to
regulate its international relations certainly must
accord them a high position among the sources of international law.

It is even harder to surmise what the PRC attitude is toward multilateral conventions as law making
instruments. In view of the fact that, until recently,
the PRC has not participated in these conventions, we
can only wait to see what the forthcoming attitude
toward this type of law making instrument will be.

Conclusion of Treaties with Non-recognizing States

The problem of non-recognition and its effect
on treaties is clearly a salient problem in regard
to the PRC. Since the culmination of the revolution
in 1949 the PRC has gradually been recognized by an
ever increasing number of the world's States. The in-

clusion of the PRC in the United Nations in October
1971 appears to have been an added motivating force
to many nations not theretofore granting recognition
to the PRC government. However, there are still a
great many governments that do not recognize and do
not have diplomatic relations with the PRC.[5] In the
past there have been nations which have concluded
treaties prior to recognizing or establishing diplomatic relations with the PRC. Currently there are
still States which have treaty commitments with the
PRC but do not recognize her or do not have diplomatic relations with her. The formality of these treaty
commitments ranges from informal non-governmental contractual relations as was the case with Japan to formal government to government treaties as with Cambodia.

The problem of non-recognition and the effect on
treaties cannot be divorced from the overall legal
effects of recognition itself. There are, of course,
certain legal criteria upon which the decision to
recognize a government or not recognize a government
or a State may be based. The legal criteria for recognition as a State pose little in the way of legal
problems. The traditional criteria for recognition of
an entity as an independent State are, the possession
of territory, the existence of a sovereign stable
government which rules supreme within that territory,

and the exercise of control by that government over
the people within its territorial confines.[6] A
government which seeks to be recognized should meet
the following criteria:

> It should be in actual control of the terri-
> tory and population with an expectation of
> durability... so as to be held responsible
> for the conduct of the state and be able to
> fulfill its international obligations.[7]

There seems little doubt that after 24 years of rule
of mainland China the People's Republic of China certainly meets all of the legal criteria for recognition as both a State and the controlling government
thereof.

In addition to, or perhaps in lieu of, the legal
criteria for recognition many States have sought to
apply political considerations in the matter of recognition. These political considerations include, among
others, the existence of free elections and the establishment of democratic principles and institutions
by the new government. These same political argu-
ments have been advanced as reasons for the non-recognition of the PRC, particularly by the United States.
B.R. Bot points out that,

> ... the U.S.A. has repeated over and over
> again that its refusal to recognize was
> to a large extent determined by the fact
> that the Communist regime lacked the posi-
> tive support of the population. The same
> arguments are invoked by many other states
> that so far have withheld the official

stamp of approval from the governments
of the DDR, North Vietnam, North Korea
and Communist China.[8]

Yet many of these countries which have not officially

recognized the PRC, including the United States, have

concluded bilateral agreements with that government

and have participated in multilateral conventions to

which the PRC has been a party. What effect, then,

does non-recognition have on the validity of these

treaties and conversely what effect does participa-

tion in bilateral and multilateral agreements with a

"non-recognized state" have on recognition, either

implicit or explicit?

Though there is no specific agreed upon rela-

tionship between treaty relations with a non-recog-

nized entity and implied recognition, a few guide-

lines have nonetheless emerged through the years.

There has been an attempt to draw guidelines concern-

ing the volume and type of contacts which may be en-

tered without implying recognition. For example it

has often been said that the conclusion of a bilateral

treaty implies recognition to the previously unrecog-

nized entity. As early as 1928 U.S. Secretary of

State Kellogg stated that "... the signing of a bila-

teral treaty ... constitutes recognition."[9]

Nonetheless, State practice has shown that

governments often enter into bilateral agreements of

a technical, specific or temporary nature with other governments which they have no intention or recognizing.[10] For example, the United States entered into the now famous Agreed Measures Announcement with the PRC on September 10, 1955. The international legal character of this "agreement" has been in doubt almost since its announcement and has given rise to charges of violations by both sides. The Agreed Measures took the form of two separate announcements made by the United States ambassador and the Chinese ambassador. The Agreed Measures were concerned with the return of United States and Chinese civilians to their respective countries.

The legal status of the Agreed Measures in U.S. practice is doubtful. It is listed neither in the official U.S. Treaties and Other International Acts nor in the Treaties in Force, published by the State Department. The PRC, on the other hand, regards this as a legally binding agreement and in fact has included it in the fourth edition of the official PRC treaty series (TYC).[11]

In spite of the fact that the United States took great care to formulate the Agreed Measures in the form of two separate announcements there is little reason to doubt that this, nonetheless, had the legal effect of creating an international agreement. B.R.

Bot has observed that,

> As to the form of the agreement it
> may be observed that, in spite of the uni-
> lateral declarations both parties have
> made, the similar wording and the recipro-
> cal obligations characterize it as a do
> ut des deal. For, it can hardly be ex-
> pected that the U.S.A. would take "appro-
> priate measures so that they (Chinese in
> the U.S.A.) can expeditiously exercise
> their right to return" if the Communist
> Chinese authorities would not, in a like
> manner, safeguard the return of Americans
> in China. Therefore it seems justified to
> hold that this agreement falls at least in
> the category of oral agreements. And this
> oral pledge has even been recorded and for
> the sake of clarity put into the form of a
> written statement. [12]

In addition to this agreement the United States
has dealt with the PRC to negotiate the Korean Armistice and the reunification of Korea. Also in 1955
the U.S. began talks, at the ambassadorial level, with
the PRC.

But, none of these agreements and negotiations
carried with them the intention to grant diplomatic
recognition to the People's Republic of China. The
historical record plus a statement by John Foster
Dulles in 1958 adequately supports this contention,

> Since August 1955 we have conducted
> negotiations at the ambassadorial level
> with them, first at Geneva and now at War-
> saw. But it is one thing to deal with the
> Chinese Communist regime in relation to
> specific problems. It is another thing
> to accord it general diplomatic recogni-
> tion. [13]

Another case involving a different type of in-

ternational obligation is the Sino-Japanese Fisheries
agreements. These agreements are in the form of contractual arrangements entered into by fisheries asso-
ciations from the two countries. They regulate all
matters concerning fishing such as delineation of
fishing zones, right to shelter in ports, etc., matters which are normally reserved for official government agencies. As with the U.S.-PRC agreement, the
PRC views these contracts as official agreements and
has included them in the official treaty series (TYC).
The Japanese Foreign Office, on the other hand, accords no official status to these agreements. However, as Lee points out,

> Just as ambassadorial talks were
> used as a substitute for normal diplo-
> matic channels between Washington and
> Peking, agreements between fisheries
> associations were utilized to take the
> place of fisheries treaties between
> Japan and the PRC.[14]

It is clear then, that in regard to State practice, governments often enter into agreements with
other governments which for one reason or another they
do not recognize and may have no intention of recognizing. It can probably be safely inferred then, that
in spite of attempts to build criteria to the contrary, bilateral agreements between non-recognizing
States and non-recognized entities do not prejudice
the non-recognizing State in favor of either implied

or stated recognition.

The converse of the above discussion, i.e. what effect does non-recognition have on the legality of treaties concluded by the PRC, can be dealt with rather succinctly by reference to the Vienna Convention on the Law of Treaties. First, it can be stated categorically that the PRC possesses all of the characteristics which qualify it for legal definition as a State; and, according to Article 6 of the Vienna Convention "Every State possesses the capacity to conclude treaties." Further, in regard to diplomatic recognition and the conclusion of treaties the Convention states inter alia,

> The severance or absence of diplomatic or consular relations between two or more States does not prevent the conclusion of treaties between those States. [15]

And conversely,

> The conclusion of a treaty does not in itself affect the situation in regard to diplomatic or consular relations. [16]

In Western practice then, all treaties concluded between States and non-recognized entities have the same legal force as treaties concluded between sovereign States.

PRC Policy Toward Recognition and Treaty Relations

Like many other attitudes and policies of the

PRC concerning both foreign and domestic affairs, their attitude and policy toward recognition can be viewed from two equally rewarding yet complementary viewpoints. First, the PRC's doctrine and practice toward recognition can be divided into several historical periods, thus giving a picture of a newly formed State articulating, in its initial stages, a tight doctrinaire theory concerning recognition and gradually developing, through a kind of maturation process, a more pragmatic stance closely resembling what might be called "normal" international recognition policy. A second perspective is to examine the divergence between theory and practice in the PRC's recognition policy; for the PRC has been guilty, on numerous occasions, of violating its own specifically articulated doctrines. This applies not just to the policy of recognition and its role in law and politics but to other international political and legal practices as well.

J.C. Hsiung has divided the PRC's recognition practices into three historical phases. The phases are, "The initial years (1949-1955), The transitional period (1956-1959), and the post 1960 period."[17] These periods can be used analogously for our analysis of PRC attitudes and practices in treaty making.

The initial period was characterized by a general tendency to minimize the importance of recognition. This was undoubtedly due, in part, to the new regime's desire to establish diplomatic and economic relations with numerous States coupled with its sensitivity over the United States' position regarding non-recognition of the PRC. With only one exception, the out-going communications from the PRC during this period omitted any reference to recognition. The one exception was Chou En-lai's response to the Soviet Union's message of October 2, 1949, in which the Soviet Union indicated a willingness to establish diplomatic relations with the PRC. Even though the Soviet Union's message made no explicit mention of recognition per se, Chou responded by thanking the Soviet government for being "the first friendly state to recognize the People's Republic of China."[18]

The doctrine followed by the PRC during this early period has come to be known as the "Mao Tsetung Doctrine." It was first articulated in Article 56 of the Common Program adopted by the Chinese People's Political Consultative Conference in 1949.[19] There were two primary stipulations in Article 56. The first was that establishment of diplomatic relations should be based on the principles of "equality, mutual benefit and mutual respect for territory and

sovereignty." And, second that nations intending to establish diplomatic relations with the PRC must "sever relations with the Kuomintang reactionary clique."[20]

During this initial stage the primary concern of the PRC government was the establishment of diplomatic and trade relations with as many States as possible. Mere recognition was accorded only a minor place in PRC international affairs. The PRC's apparent concern over recognition was so secondary to the desire to establish diplomatic relations, that when Israel and Afghanistan recognized the PRC, the new regime merely thanked them for their decision.[21]

The PRC departed radically from custom in only one aspect of their recognition practice during this phase. It has been customary in international practime that if any conditions are to be attached at the time of recognition they will be attached by the recognizing State. The PRC departed from this practice by always insisting on ad hoc negotiations, following the recognition, and prior to the establishment of diplomatic relations. This held, according to Hsiung, except when, "the recognizing state was from the Communist bloc" or "when a state merely recognized Peking but professed no interest in having diplomatic ties."[22]

Also during this initial period, the first occasion arose in which the PRC had the opportunity to be the recognizing State. Three new governments came into being during this period. They were, the German Democratic Republic in October, 1949, the Democratic Republic of Vietnam in January, 1950 and Indonesia in March, 1950. On each occasion Chou En-lai sent congratulatory messages acknowledging the governments; but, as in all other outgoing communications no mention was made of recognition.[23]

During the transitional period from 1956-1959, with the emergence of many new Afro-Asian States the PRC began to modify its practice and began to explicitly "recognize" several of the new States. The first State to be accorded such privilege was the Republic of Sudan on January 4, 1956.[24] This period, which was characterized by a general relaxation of the PRC's attitude toward recognition, according to James C. Hsuing, reflected the PRC's attempt to,

> ...circumvent the impact of the United States nonrecognition through the cultivation of friendship with the nonaligned states. Although similar attempts had been made before, as in Peking's "unofficial" trade relations with Japan, the 1956-1959 period saw a more self-assured CPR extending its contacts from the immediate surrounding regions to the Middle East, Africa, and other parts of the world.[25]

Since 1960 the PRC has followed a rather consistent formula in acknowledgment and recognition of new governments. Chou En-lai would offer felicitations and Foreign Minister Ch'en Yi would extend express recognition by the PRC government.[26] Also during this most recent period of development in the PRC's recognition practices there appeared a rather systematic discussion of the question of recognition practices by K'ung Meng in a 1960 article entitled "A Critique of the Bourgeois International Law Regarding 'Subjects of International Law' and Theories of Recognition of States."[27] In this article K'ung condemns the withholding of recognition for political purposes. He considers this practice to be a form of aggression by the non-recognizing State. The article equally condemns premature recognition. K'ung asserts that,

> After the establishment of the capitalist system, the theory of bourgeois international law concerning recognition, combined with its theory concerning subjects of international law, became an instrument for coping with independence movements in colonies and semicolonies and socialist revolution in various countries.

and further that,

> ... although recognition of a new state or a new government is a unilateral political act on the part of the recognizing state, on the other hand, recognition is also a system of international law and should not violate the generally

recognized principles of international
law. That is to say that no state should
use recognition as an instrument of its
aggressive policy or resort to premature
recognition or delayed recognition to
acquire illegal interests or to realize
its object of aggression.[28]

The author also attacks the "constitutive" theory

of recognition as an inspiration of the capitalistic

community. He characterizes the "constitutive" the-

ory as an attempt by those in power to suppress the

new nations through bourgeois methods. While the

article does not specifically defend the "declaratory"

theory of recognition the implications in that direc-

tion are clear.[29] This particular stance by the PRC

is in keeping with a recent trend in international law

which favors the declaratory theory over the older

constitutive theory. This trend has, in no small

part, been a result of the rapid proliferation of new

nation-states and revolutionary regimes since World

War II. The declaratory theory, which states in es-

sence, that a new State or government becomes a sub-

ject of international law, irrespective of recognition,

when qualifications of statehood have been met, is not

far removed from the current PRC doctrine on recogni-

tion. Certainly the PRC view that condemns the with-

holding or premature granting of recognition for poli-

tical purposes finds a great deal of support in West-

ern international law.

Following this particular line of reasoning the
PRC has particularly attacked the United States for
its efforts at preventing other nations from recognizing the PRC. In the same article K'ung Meng charges
that,

> The pressure exercised by strong imperi-
> alist countries upon other countries to
> force them to recognize or not recognize
> certain new countries or governments
> (such as the United States' pressure on
> other countries to withhold recognition
> of China) is a serious illegal act.[30]

There is no doubt some truth in the PRC charges.
In fact, as B.R. Bot notes, the United States may
have been guilty of an _abus de droit_ not only in its
own recognition policies but in attempting to coerce
other nations, through various means, to not recognize the PRC.[31] One can assert with a reasonable degree of certainty that until recently Japan's policy
of non-recognition toward the PRC had been motivated,
in large part, by implicit (or perhaps explicit) economic threat from the United States.

While the PRC's doctrine of recognition is compatible with Western theory, her actions often are
not. Though condemning the practice herself, in
theory through the writings of Party oriented scholars, the PRC has often recognized revolutionary regimes prematurely. The most notable case perhaps,
was the PRC's recognition of the Algerian Provi-

sional Government three days after its formation in
1958, while it still had its headquarters in Cairo.[32]
This and other cases have lead one author to remark
that the PRC may often be recognizing new regimes
"de ideologia."[33] This of course is not entirely un-
known in Western practice. The United States, for
example, as early as the beginning of the Panamanian
Republic, has used premature recognition to further
political ends.[34]

Although the PRC seems to be guilty of the practice of premature recognition when revolutionary
groups are striving for power, there do not seem to be
any cases where recognition has been withheld for political purposes.

In sum then, the PRC does not divagate far from
either Western theory or Western practice when it
comes to recognition policies, though in both cases
theory and practice often do not coincide. The PRC
carries on treaty, trade and other relations with
both recognizing and non-recognizing States, her main
concerns in current practice being based on pragmatic
rather than legal or ideological considerations.

The PRC and the Matter of State Succession to Treaties

Another particular problem that has been of
great interest concerning the PRC is a concept known,

not altogether appropriately, as the "law of State succession."[35] That is, when one government supercedes
another, by any one of a number of means, including
violent revolution, to what extent do the privileges,
and ipso facto the obligations, of the former government devolve upon the new regime?

In Western practice the attitude toward this
problem has been mixed. Some Western scholars have
accepted as a general principle that the validity of
a State's obligations are not altered as a result of
a change in government.[36]

The problem over the continuity or discontinuity
of the international personality of a State arises in
situations of territorial changes, belligerent occupation (short of debellatio), and revolution. In the
latter case it is generally assumed that the matter
is of internal concern, is totally within the domestic jurisdiction of the State, and thus has no effect
on the international personality of the State.[37]

This particular view is based on the generally
accepted principle of the continuity of the State as
an international personality; since the fact of international personality supersedes concerns over form of
government, obligations devolve on the new government
providing the State remains intact. In support of
this line of reasoning D.P. O'Connell states,

> Change in government does not affect the
> personality of the State, and hence a
> successor government is required by in-
> ternational law to perform the obliga-
> tions undertaken on behalf of the State
> by its predecessor.[38]

Judicial decisions which also support this par-

ticular view are the cases of The Sapphire and Lehigh

Valley R.R. vs. The State of Russia. Both cases held

inter alia that the State continued irrespective of

changes in government and irrespective of the method

of change.[39]

However, all are not in total agreement with

this particular view, which might be faulted for at-

tempting to oversimplify an extremely complex issue.

Schwarzenberger, for example, states that "... it

would be unsafe to abstract from rather scanty evi-

dence a general rule of subrogation or State succes-

sion."[40]

Probably the most complex treatment of State

succession is given by the Soviets. It was they in

fact, in 1917, who were among the first to challenge

the idea of general State succession to treaties. At

that time the Soviet Union maintained its right to

abrogate, unilaterally, certain treaties negotiated

by the preceding government. The Soviets justified

their stance by maintaining that the abrogated trea-

ties were either "unequal treaties" or were agree-

ments representing intervention against Soviet Russia

in support of the Tsarist government, and they thus should be annulled.[41] The Soviet views on the matter of State succession, which are expressed in a recent Soviet text on international law, treat the problem as having different ramifications dependent upon the method by which the new government or State came into being.[42]

The category of succession most relevant to both the Soviet Union and the PRC is "Succession Following the Replacement of a State of One Historical Type by That of Another." The text states that with this particular type of succession the

> State which emerges as a result of social revolution and which, in class character, constitutes a State of a new type is unconditionally the full successor of the extinct State regarding all territories and all properties, both on the territory of the given State and on the territories of other States.[43]

However with respect to treaties, which of course imply obligations and duties on the part of the successor State, the attitude seems quite different. The Soviet text states,

> The question of succession as regards the treaty obligations of the former State, including obligations of a political, economic and financial (loans) character, is more complex. In this case, succession cannot be considered as coming of itself, insofar as a qualitatively new subject of International Law has appeared. The new State itself determines its attitude to the treaties concluded by its predecessor,

customarily making the appropriate
declarations to this effect.[44]

The significant theoretical distinction that exists between the Western and Soviet doctrines is, of
course, the attribution of continuance or discontinu-
ance of the international personality of the State.
Obviously based on Marxian principles, the Soviet idea
of the creation of a new State and the extinction of
the old emphasizes the differences in "historical
type," thus giving them theoretical grounds for the
claim to have created a new State ab intra with a distinct international personality, irrespective of the
fact that the new State's territorial confines were
coextensive with those of the former State.

The PRC also has apparently followed the Soviet
doctrine that the succeeding State or government may
reserve for itself the right to continue or abrogate
treaties on a selective basis. They also more or
less consider themselves to have created a new Chinese
State as a result of the revolution.[45]

The Common Program of The Chinese People's Political Consultative Conference, adopted at the First
Plenary Session of CPPCC on September 29, 1949 in Peking, addresses the problem of succession to treaties
concluded by the former government. Article 55, Chapter VII of the Common Program states that

> The Central People's Government of the
> People's Republic of China shall ex-
> amine the treaties and agreements con-
> cluded between the Kuomintang and for-
> eign governments, and shall recognize,
> abrogate, revise or re-negotiate them
> according to their respective contents.[46]

Although this particular statement mentions only those treaties concluded by the Kuomintang government, PRC practice has shown that it considers the substance of the statement to include those treaties concluded by the pre-Nationalist government as well. It has also recently been applied to some of the treaties concluded by Imperial China.

This particular point of view has indeed caused difficulties for the PRC among the other nations of the world, even those recognizing the Communists as the legitimate government of China. Several Western States, that recognized the PRC quite early, consider that treaties signed before 1949 are still in force. The Netherlands, for example, recognized the PRC in 1950[47] and considers that the PRC is still bound by 4 treaties concluded between China and the Netherlands prior to 1949.[48]

According to one author, officials of the Dutch Ministry of Foreign Affairs have expressed serious doubt about the validity of the treaties.[49] In fact, one of the treaties, an Arbitration Agreement of 1916, has specifically been denounced by the PRC. They have

been mute concerning the other three but do not abide
by their provisions.

The United Kingdom and France, both of which have
recognized the PRC, have had similar experiences in
their treaty negotiations with that government.
France apparently still considers the treaties made
with the former government to be in force. The United
Kingdom, on the other hand, has omitted these treaties from its more recent treaty series publications
and thus apparently accepts the unilateral abrogation
by the PRC as a fait accompli.[50]

Article 56 of the Common Program further clari-
fies the PRC's intentions with respect to the renegotiation or continuance of any treaties signed prior
to its coming to power. It states that,

> The Central People's Government of the
> People's Republic of China may on the
> basis of equality, mutual benefit and
> mutual respect for territory and sover-
> eignty negotiate with foreign govern-
> ments which have severed relations with
> the Kuomintang reactionary clique and
> which adopt a friendly attitude toward
> the People's Republic of China...[51]

Since, unilateral abrogation of treaties is not
an accepted practice in international law and since
international law and relations are based on the principle of reciprocity, the PRC has in most instances
renegotiated agreements with those States which recognize her in accordance with Article 56 of the Common

Program.

One striking example of the PRC's insistence on
the provision of a recognizing government's severing
relations with the "Kuomintang reactionary clique"
came in 1964 when France decided to recognize the PRC.
She did so in the hope of maintaining relations with
"both Chinas." Peking was adamant however, and
France finally yielded by breaking off official relations with Nationalist China.[52]

In the matter of multilateral treaties the PRC
policy has been quite consistent with that of its
bilateral arrangements. That is, it refuses to become a party to any agreement to which the Nationalist
government is a party. It does, however, seem to consider that multilateral treaties, especially those
which establish international organizations, should
continue in force with respect to the State, irrespective of revolutionary changes in government.

The PRC's insistence that it be seated in the
United Nations in place of the Nationalist government
is but one example bearing out this premise. In addition to the United Nations itself, Peking sent nine
cables to various related organs of the U.N. between
October 1, 1949 and June 30, 1950, all concerned with
PRC representation in those organs and their legal
position on the matter.[53]

There are only two existing multilateral treaties to which both Chinese governments are parties.
The first is the Geneva Protocol of 1925 Prohibiting
the Use in War of Asphyxiating, Poisonous or Other
Gases and of Biological Methods of Warfare.[54]   Nationalist China acceded to this Protocol on August 7,
1929.[55]   The PRC, in a statement by Chou En-lai on
July 13, 1952, recognized the agreement.[56]   There was
apparently no demand for the withdrawal of the Nationalist accession.[57]

The only other multilateral convention to which
both the Nationalists and Communists are parties is
the 1930 Load Line Convention.[58]   This Convention,
like the Geneva Protocol, was acceded to by the Nationalists initially and later accepted by the PRC.[59]
Again no pressure was exerted by the PRC to have the
Nationalist accession replaced.[60]   On all other multilateral treaties only one of the contending governments is a party.

The general situation regarding the matter of
State succession and the People's Republic of China
is, of course, further complicated by the continuing
existence of the Nationalist Chinese government of
Taiwan.   Moreover, this is not just a typical case of
a government in exile, pretending, as it were, to the
throne.   The complexity of the issue has been exacer-

bated by the extent to which both governments actually
occupy and control a portion of that territory which
each claims to be a legal part of the whole of China.
That the PRC controls a vastly greater portion of China than the Nationalists is of no real consequence in
the resolution of the theoretical-legal problem.

Except for the insistence of both regimes that
there is and can be only one China, (for which both
claim to be the rightful government), the rest of the
world would probably have accepted a "two Chinas policy" some time ago. Certainly there have been plenty
of examples of nations making an attempt at a "two
Chinas solution" to support this assertion in spite
of Chinese insistence to the contrary.

This perhaps would have been an easy solution to
the problem of succession to treaties. The Nationalists could have continued as party to all treaties
signed by them (with the obvious exception of treaties
specific to territory such as boundary treaties) and
the PRC would have been free to renegotiate their own
bilateral settlements and accede to the multilateral
treaties of their own choosing. Instead the world
has been faced with one China - two governments, at
the insistence of the rivals.

Unequal Treaties
The concept in treaty law subscribed to by the

PRC that is probably most divergent from Western
practice is that of "unequal treaties." The term "unequal treaties" is not an invention by the Chinese
Communist regime but has been known for centuries in
China, Japan, Russia and in Western international law.

The concept was discussed in Western international law by such early writers as, Grotius, Pufendorf, Vattel and Wolff.[61] The idea of unequal treaties
as discussed by these classical theorists, however,
differs greatly from both the PRC's concept and that
understood in earlier China and Japan. For example,
none of these writers considered that inequality in
treaties was in any way a cause for abrogation or a
factor invalidating treaties. Most authors merely
acknowledged the fact that treaties could be made on
either equal or unequal terms. Vattel did venture
to argue that out of a sense of justice, nations
"should make their treaties equal, as far as that is
possible."[62]

Thus the extent to which Classical Western writers have treated the concept of unequal treaties,
and the theoretical content thereof, is of only peri-
pheral, historical interest to the modern concept of
unequal treaties applied by the PRC. Since the nineteenth century Western interest in unequal treaties
has waned. In fact we fail to find this concept even

mentioned by most twentieth century Western legal
scholars.[63]

Though not treated theoretically, the concept of
unequal treaties came to be of some interest in the
early twentieth century when the Soviet Union offered
to abolish many of the treaties imposed on Asian
States by Tsarist Russia. Also during this period
the pre-Nationalist government of China was attempting
to abrogate many of the unequal treaties that had
been forced on Imperial China.

The term "unequal treaties" as used by pre-Nationalist China and Nationalist China referred to
those treaties that had been forced on China by the
Western powers, Russia and Japan during the nineteenth
and early twentieth centuries. These treaties, as
described in Chapter I above, exacted many concessions from China in the form of unilateral and broad-
scoped most-favored-nation treatment, extraterritorial jurisdiction in civil and military cases, re-
strictive tariff regulations, territorial cessions
and lease arrangements.[64]

Though the pre-Nationalist government made
serious attempts to rid China of these treaties these
efforts were ineffective. It was not until 1928,
when the Kuomintang government of Chiang Kai-shek
unilaterally announced the termination of all expired

unequal treaties and the renegotiation of all other
treaties on the basis of sovereignty and equality,
that effective steps were begun to relieve the burden
of these unequal treaties.[65] The announcement resulted, not from a sudden turn of events for the Chinese,
but rather was inspired by a growing revolutionary
and nationalistic fervor. This newborn nationalism
was fueled by various and diverse internal and external events such as China's "betrayal" at the Versailles Convention and the killing of demonstrating
students by foreign police in Shanghai.[66] These and
other events caused strong contemptuous feelings
among the youth and the new elite for the servitude
that had been imposed on China by the unequal treaties.[67]

The Second World War was an untimely intervention in the Nationalist Chinese attempt to renegotiate
for new treaties. But shortly after the end of the
war they succeeded, to their satisfaction, in abrogating all unequal treaties that had been imposed on
Imperial China.[68]

Currently both the Soviet Union and the PRC subscribe to the notion of unequal treaties and their
invalidity. A recent Soviet international law text
states that,

> Equal treaties are treaties concluded on
> the basis of the equality of the parties;

> unequal treaties are those which do not
> fulfill this elementary requirement.
> Unequal treaties are not legally bind-
> ing; equal treaties must be strictly ob-
> served.[69]

and further,

> It has already been noted that un-
> equal treaties and treaties of similar
> character are not binding. Their an-
> nulment does not contradict generally
> recognized democratic principles of pre-
> sent-day International Law.[70]

It is clear from these statements that the So-

viets consider one primary attribute as the determi-

nant for classification of treaties into equal and un-

equal categories. That factor is the equality of the

States concerned in the negotiations. It is unclear

whether or not this concept applies equally to bila-

teral and multilateral treaties. In addition there is

no specification as to the criteria for determining

the relative inqualities of the parties. Presumably

then, carrying the theme through logically to a re-

ductio ad absurdum there are possibly no treaties

which can be called "equal" under the Soviet theory.

The PRC's view of unequal treaties exceeds the

Soviet view in both complexity and political ramifi-

cations. But, the Chinese are certainly in agreement

with the Soviets on the invalidity of unequal treaties.

A Chinese text on international trade treaties com-

pares quite closely with the Soviet text cited above

on the subject of unequal treaties. It states,

> The classical writers of Marxism-Leninism
> confirmed an important principle concern-
> ing international treaties, namely, the
> genuine sovereign equality between all
> parties concerned should become the foun-
> dation of international treaties. Lenin
> said: Negotiation can only be conducted
> between equals and, therefore, genuine
> equality between both sides is an essen-
> tial condition for reaching a genuine
> agreement.
>
> Consequently, in accordance with
> Marxism-Leninsm, there are equal treaties
> and unequal treaties, and, therefore,
> progressive mankind takes fundamentally
> different attitudes towards different kinds
> of treaties. Equal treaties should be
> strictly observed. Unequal treaties are
> in violation of international law and
> without legal validity.[71]

Like the Soviet Union, the PRC is of the opinion that

unequal treaties can be <u>unilaterally</u> abrogated <u>at any</u>

<u>time</u> and that this is not contrary to the principles

of international law.

In the PRC theory of unequal treaties there are

two separate characteristics that can cause a treaty

to be classified as unequal. The first, in agreement

with the Soviet view, is the inequality of the nego-

tiating States. The second is the creation, by sub-

stantive content of the treaty, of dissimilar and non-

reciprocal obligations.[72]

The PRC has given, in part, some clarification on

the issue of inequality of parties beyond that given

by the Soviets. They have included, in the concept,

the ideas of coercion and exploitation. This parti-

cular aspect of the determinants of unequal treaties

coincides neatly with the issue of coercion in Western international law. Article 52 of the 1969 Vienna
Convention on the Law of Treaties states,

> A treaty is void if its conclusion has
> been procured by the threat or use of
> force in violation of the principles
> of international law embodied in the
> Charter of the United Nations.[73]

The convention in its Final Act also adopted a
"Declaration on the Prohibition of Military, Political or Economic Coercion in the Conclusion of Treaties." The declaration notes that, "in the past
States have sometimes been coerced to conclude treaties under pressure exerted in various forms by other
States" (emphasis added). As a result of this and
other considerations paragraph 1 of the declaration

> Solemnly condemns the threat or use
> of pressure in any form, whether military,
> political, or economic, by any State in
> order to coerce another State to perform
> any act relating to the conclusion of a
> treaty in violation of the principles of
> the sovereign equality of States and free-
> dom of consent;[74]

It would seem then, that in this particular aspect of unequal treaties, PRC practice does not differ in any great degree from the accepted practice of
the Western States. What difference there may be is
nominal and not substantive.

It should be noted that by virtue of Article 4
of the Convention, concerning its non-retroactivity,
the declaration was intended to apply only to trea-

ties concluded in the future. The PRC, as well as the Soviet Union, however, considers that the principles contained in the declaration are based on long accepted standards of international law and are therefore applicable to all treaties past, present and future.[75] The Soviet Union was a party to the Vienna Convention though the PRC was not.

Beyond the concept of coercion, which seems fairly clearly defined, other PRC criteria for the determination of equality of States seem just as murky, or absent, as those of the Soviet Union.

On the matter of substantive textual inequalities the PRC is quite clear that treaties should be based on "equal" and "reciprocal" considerations. Moreover, PRC scholars maintain that mere "verbal reciprocity" does not necessarily make a treaty "equal." They contend that relevant political and economic facts must also be taken into consideration.[76] According to Wang Yao-t'ien,

> Whether a treaty is equal does not de-
> pend upon the form and words of vari-
> ous treaty provisions, but depends
> upon the state character, economic
> strength, and the substance of corre-
> lation of the contracting states.[77]

As a result of these particular interpretations of inequality in treaties the PRC has denounced not only treaties signed by the Nationalist government but has also denounced other treaties to which they

were not party.

Among those treaties to which the PRC was not party but which it has denounced as unequal are, the 1956
United States-Swiss Agreement on Cooperation in Civil
Use of Atomic Energy,[78] The Anglo-Jordanian Alliance
Treaty of 1946,[79] The United States-Chinese Status of
Forces Agreement of 1965,[80] The 1946 United States-
Philippine Trade Agreement,[81] the United States-Ja-
pan Mutual Security Treaty of 1951[82] and the October
16, 1948 agreement between the Soviet Union and Czechoslovakia.[83] The reasons for the PRC denunciations
were wide and varied, ranging from non-reciprocal
arrangements such as the import restrictions placed
on Philippine goods by the United States, to actual
coercion as in the Soviet - Czech treaty. All, nonetheless, fell under the general rubric "unequal treaties" according to the PRC.

Nor does the PRC confine itself to the categorization of bilateral arrangements as unequal treaties.
This too is in marked contrast to the Nationalist
Chinese and Soviet practice in this area. The PRC has
denounced both the 1963 Partial Nuclear Test Ban Treaty[84] and the 1968 Treaty of Non-Proliferation of Nuclear Weapons.[85] The latter treaty was denounced as
unequal on the basis that non-nuclear States were
"...totally deprived of their right to develop nuclear

weapons for self-defense...", while on the other hand the United States and the Soviet Union, "... undertake no commitment whatsoever not to use nuclear weapons against the non-nuclear states."[86]

But, as Hungdah Chiu has aptly pointed out, the PRC does not apply the doctrine of "identical and reciprocal" obligations universally to multilateral conventions.[87] For example, the PRC has never suggested that the so-called veto power granted in the U.N. Charter, to the five permanent members of the security council, has any aspect of a non-identical and/or non-reciprocal character. In fact, it has even attacked alleged attempts by the United States to abrogate that veto power.[88] As in other areas, PRC practice does not always coincide with their doctrine.

The PRC, however, does consider the concept of unequal treaties and that of equal and reciprocal obligations seriously in its own bilateral treaty dealings. A few examples will serve to illustrate PRC sincerity in the adherence to this concept.

The first is the 1960 Sino-Burmese Boundary Treaty, which was negotiated with great care in order to preclude the possibility of any accusations arising which would place the PRC in a position resembling great power dominance.[89] China has also concluded several other boundary treaties with Nepal,[90] Pakistan,[91] Afghanistan[92] and Mongolia.[93] According to

Luke T. Lee,

> ...all these treaties appear to have
> been concluded on the basis of fair
> play and equality, and implemented
> through careful negotiating and sur-
> veying, with due regard to histori-
> cal boundaries, custom and particu-
> lar needs of the contracting parties. [94]

In other words they were, in PRC parlance, "equal

treaties."

Another case where the PRC found itself involved

in a non-reciprocal arrangement, on the beneficiary

side, was the agreement governing Sino-Indo-Chinese

relations signed on February 28, 1946. [95] The agree-

ment called for free passage of goods between Vietnam

and China, but also granted an unreciprocal right for

China to create a special zone under exclusive Chinese

jurisdiction for warehousing and docking facilities.

Though this created what certainly might be construed

as an unequal obligation, the PRC has not insisted on its

being carried out in its relations with the Democratic

Republic of Vietnam. Nor does the TYC yield any trea-

ty with such provisions. In fact the April 12, 1957

agreement between the PRC and North Vietnam concerning

customs-free transit of goods conspicuously omitted any

provision calling for such a special zone. [96]

These examples however, are not to suggest that

the PRC's record is entirely faultless in the matter

of non-reciprocal arrangements with lesser powers.

Hungdah Chiu cites the 1960 Sino-Burmese Treaty of
Friendship and Mutual Non-Aggression[97] as creating
a _de_ _facto_ non-reciprocal privilege for the PRC,
while at the same time, giving the appearance of reciprocity through what the Chinese themselves termed
mere "verbal reciprocity."[98] Chiu's point is well
taken as the treaty commits the respective contracting
parties" ... not to take part in any military alliance
against the other Contracting Party." Given the existing size and power differentials the implications of
such verbal reciprocity are clear.

The PRC has not always followed a logical and consistent pattern in the abrogation of treaties under
the unequal treaties principle. This has caused charges to be levelled at the PRC on numerous occasions
for treaty violations and has lent credence to the accusations that the PRC is an international outlaw.[99]

It is true that political considerations, apparently more frequently than legal ones, motivate the
PRC in the application of this concept. A case in
point is the Sino-Soviet boundary treaties which were
signed between Imperial China and Tsarist Russia between 1858 and 1881.[100] These treaties were not ques-
tioned by the PRC until the escalation of the Sino-
Soviet rift in the early 1960's. Then between 1962
and 1964 the PRC frequently charged that the treaties

of Aigun, Peking and Ili were unequal treaties and
therefore should be abolished and renegotiated.[101]
One author has noted that these particular tirades indicated the seriousness of the Sino-Soviet conflict
during this time.[102]

There seems little doubt that there is some basis for the PRC claims, as these treaties were forced
on the Chinese Empire by Russia; however, it is also
clear that the motivation behind the charges was contemporary and political rather than historical and
legal.[103]

It is easy to conclude then, that since the PRC
does act on the basis of political motivation in the
application of the unequal treaty concept, and since
the concept itself is theoretically rather unclear,
that they have merely constructed a legal deus ex
machina in order to extricate themselves from difficult or unmitigable situations.

In the opinion of this author this does nothing
to set the PRC apart from other States which may be
champions of the Western system of international law.
It has been shown quite convincingly that Western
States often use international law merely to cloak
otherwise questionable acts in a mantle of legality,
or in crisis times may abandon it altogether except
perhaps for the mere payment of lip service.[104] The

exploitation of the unequal treaty concept by the PRC
then, should not be altogether surprising.

A politically parallel concept in Western international law might be clausula rebus sic stantibus.
Although this concept has been a much debated issue
by Western legal scholars it has been included in the
Vienna Convention of the Law of Treaties. Article 62
of the Convention, titled "Fundamental change of circumstances," cites two instances where rebus sic stantibus may be "invoked as a ground for terminating or
withdrawing from the treaty ..."[105]

It has long been known that invocations of rebus
sic stantibus like invocations of unequal treaties
are quite often politically motivated. Oliver Lissitzyn notes in this regard that

> Its practical importance may at times be
> exaggerated; but nations dissatisfied
> with the status quo continue to regard it
> as a welcome device for escaping burdensome
> treaties, while others fear it as a threat
> to stability and to their interests.[106]

The point here is not to attempt to compare the
legalities involved in these two obviously diverse
concepts but rather to indicate that each legal concept has its own untenable aspects and, further, that
each often becomes a basis for politically motivated
change in the status quo.

Finally, it is interesting to note that the idea
of unequal treaties has recently been picked up by

several of the newly emerging and developing nations.
They have used the concepts of inequality in treaties,
and duress to claim similarly that treaties falling
into either of these categories are void ab initio.[107]
Thus it would appear that an ancient concept, revived
by the PRC, has possibilities of gaining rather wide
acceptance, especially among those nations known as
the "third world."

FOOTNOTES

1. F.I. Kozhevnikov, ed., International Law, Moscow, Foreign Languages Publishing House, n.d., p.12.

2. Wei Liang, "On Post Second World War International Treaties," Kuo-chi t'iao-yueh chi, 1953-1955, (International Treaty Series), Peking, Shih-chieh chih-shih ch'u-pan she, 1961, p. 660.

3. Wang Yao-t'ien, Kuo-chi mao-yi t'iao-yueh ho hsieh-ting, (International Trade Treaties and Agreements), Peking, Ts'ai-cheng ching-chi ch'u-pan she, 1958, p. 10.

4. Ying T'ao, "Recognize the True Face of Bourgeois International Law from a Few Basic Concepts," Kuo-chi wen-t'i yen-chiu (Studies in International Problems), No. 1, (January, 1960), p. 47, translated in Jerome A. Cohen and Hungdah Chiu, People's China and International Law: A Documentary Study, Princeton, Princeton University Press, 1974, pp. 70-72.

5. Since the PRC took the "China seat" in the United Nations in 1971 it has been recognized by an additional 13 nations. This brings to 73 the total of nations maintaining diplomatic relations with the PRC by 1974.

6. B.R. Bot, Nonrecognition and Treaty Relations, Leyden, A.W. Sijthoff, 1968, p. 21; also see Georg Schwarzenberger, A Manual of International Law, New York, Praeger, 1967, p. 55.

7. Bot, op. cit., p. 21.

8. Ibid., p. 25; also see Quincy Wright, "The Chinese Recognition Problem," American Journal of International Law, Vol. 49, no. 3, (July, 1955) pp. 325-326; and C.G. Fenwick, "The Recognition of the Communist Government of China," American Journal of International Law, Vol. 47, No. 4, (October, 1953,) pp. 659-660.

9. Bot, op. cit., p. 30.

10. Ibid.

11. TYC 4:1

12. Bot, op. cit., p. 95.

13. John Foster Dulles, "Challenge for Peace in the Far East," Department of State Bulletin, No. 39, (1958), p. 561.

14. Luke T. Lee, China and International Agreements, Durham, N.C., Rule of Law Press, p. 61.

15. Vienna Convention, International Legal Materials, Vol. VIII, No. 4, (July, 1969) p. 707.

16. Ibid.

17. See James C. Hsiung. Law and Policy in China's Foreign Relations, New York, Columbia University Press, 1972, pp. 205-227 for an in depth treatment of this subject.

18. Chou's complete reply to Soviet Foreign Minister Gromyko may be found in Chung-hua jen-min kung-ho-kuo tui-wai kuan -hsi wen-chien chi, (Collection of Documents Relating to the People's Republic of China), Vol. I, (1949), pp. 5-6. Quoted in Hsiung, op.cit.,p.206.

19. The English translation of the full text of the Common Program may be found in Albert P. Blaustein, ed., Fundamental Legal Documents of Communist China, South Hackensack, New Jersey, Rothman,1962,pp.34-53.

20. Ibid. Article 56, p.53; The doctrine was also articulated by Mao Tse-tung on October 1, 1949. The text of Mao's proclamation along with Chou En-lai's transmittal thereof may be found in TWKH Vol. I,(1949) pp. 3-5.

21. Hsiung, op. cit., p. 207; The full text of the announcements can be found in TWKH Vol. I,(1949), pp. 22-24.

22. Hsiung, op. cit., p. 208.

23. Ibid., p. 210.

24. Recognitions by the PRC in the form of announcements are recorded in TWKH for corresponding year.

25. Hsiung, op. cit., p. 212.

26. The English translations of these messages are recorded in SCMP for the corresponding year. See for example, the recognition of Togo on April 27, 1960 in SCMP, No. 2249, p. 54.

27. K'ung Meng, "A Critique of the Bourgois In-

ternational Law Regarding Subjects of International Law," KCWTYC, Vol. 2, (1960), pp. 44-53.

28. K'ung Meng, op. cit., pp. 51-53, translated in Cohen and Chiu, op. cit., pp. 246-250. Cohen and Chiu, in response to K'ung's remarks, have noted that although K'ung "undoubtedly would not concede that the PRC has ever violated his strictures against the use of recognition for aggressive or otherwise illegal purposes, the PRC has plainly denied recognition for political purposes", see Cohen and Chiu, op. cit., p. 250.

29. Ibid., pp. 247-248; also Hsiung, op. cit., p.219; for a full discussion of the "constitutive" and "declaratory" theories on recognition see Bot., op. cit., pp. 16-21 and passim. Also for a discussion of a slightly modified constitutive theory see H. Lauterpacht, Recognition in International Law, Cambridge, Harvard University Press, 1948, p. 40.

30. K'ung Meng, op. cit., p. 53; translated in Cohen and Chiu, op. cit., p. 250.

31. Bot., op. cit., p. 52.

32. Hsiung, op. cit., p. 221.

33. Ibid., p. 222.

34. See Edwin C. Hoyt, National Policy and International Law: Case Studies from American Canal Policy, Monograph Series in World Affairs Vol. 4, No. 1, Denver, Colorado, Denver University Press, 1966-67, pp. 31-32.

35. Schwarzenberger, op. cit., p. 89.

36. L. Oppenheim, International Law, Vol. I, 8th ed., Lauterpacht, London, Longmans, Green, 1955, pp. 948-949.

37. Schwarzenberger, op. cit., p. 86.

38. D.P. O'Connell, International Law, Vol. I, London, Stevens, 1965, p. 456.

39. For a discussion of The Sapphire Case see, Friedmann, Lissitzyn and Pugh, eds., International Law: Cases and Materials, St. Paul, West, 1969, pp. 199-200. For a discussion of Lehigh Valley R.R. v. The

State of Russia see Hsiung, op. cit., p. 215.

40. Schwarzenberger, op. cit., p. 89; for further discussion see Okon Udokang, Succession of New
States to International Treaties, Dobbs Ferry, Oceana,
1972.

41. Kozhevnikov, op. cit., pp. 125-126.

42. Ibid., pp. 125-130. The categories listed
are: 1. Succession following the replacement of a
State of one historical type by that of another; 2.
Succession of States emerging as a result of the National Liberation Struggle; 3. Succession when two
or more States merge or the breaking up of a State into different States.

43. Kozhevnikov, op. cit., p. 125.

44. Ibid.

45. Bot, op. cit., p. 194.

46. Supra note 19.

47. The text of the recognition announcement is
found in the Yearbook of the Dutch Ministry of Foreign
Affairs 1949-1950, p. 150. Also cited in Bot, op. cit,
p. 23.

48. The four treaties which are mentioned in
Stuyt, Repertorium van door Nederland tussen 1813 en
1950 gesloten Verdragen are: Treaty of Friendship and
Commerce, October 6, 1863, (No. 424), p. 114; Consular Agreement, May 8, 1916 (No. 1124), p. 153; Arbitration Agreement, June 1, 1915 (No. 1195) p. 158;
and the Treaty for Regulation of Tariff Relations,
Dec. 19, 1928 (No. 1560), p. 191. All of the above
cited agreements are cited in Bot, op. cit., p. 195.

49. Bot, op. cit., p. 195.

50. For a discussion of treaty relations between
the United Kingdom and the PRC see Bot, op. cit., pp.
47,48,101,195.

51. Blaustein, op. cit., p. 53.

52. Bot, op. cit., p. 49; for a further discussion representing the PRC's attitude concerning "two
China's" see Shao Chin-fu, "The Absurd Theory of 'Two

China's' and Principles of International Law," KCWTYC
No. 2, 1959, pp. 8-12; translated in Oppose the New
U.S. Plots to Create "Two Chinas," Peking, Foreign
Language Press, 1962; the article also appears in
Cohen and Chiu, op. cit., pp. 231-237.

53. Byron S.J. Weng, Peking's U.N. Policy: Continuity and Change, New York, Praeger, 1972, p. 78.

54. LNTS 94:65.

55. Ibid. p. 71

56. TYC 6:320

57. Hungdah Chiu, The People's Republic of China
and the Law of Treaties, Cambridge, Harvard University
Press, 1972, p. 94.

58. TYC 6:282, LNTS 135:301.

59. The text of the Nationalist Accession is in
LNTS 160:417. The PRC acceptance does not appear in
the TYC.

60. Chiu, op. cit., p. 95.

61. H. Grotius, De jure belli ac pacis, (On the
Law of War and Peace) translated by F.W. Kelsey from
1646 ed. Vol. II, Washington, D.C., Carnegie Endowment
for International Peace, 1925, p. 394; Samuel Pufendorf, De jure naturae et gentium, (On the Law of Nature and Nations), Vol. II, Translated by C.H. Oldfather and W.A. Oldfather from 1688 ed., Washington,
D.C., Carnegie Endowment for International Peace, 1934;
E. Vattel, Le Droit des gens: au principes de la loi
naturelle, (The Law of Nations or the Principles of Natural Law), Translated by C.G. Fenwick from 1758 ed.,
Vol. III, Washington, D.C., Carnegie Endowment for International Peace, 1916, p. 165; Christian von Wolff,
Jus gentium methodo scientifica pertratatum, (The Law
of Nations Treated According to the Scientific Method),
Translated by Drake from 1764 ed., Washington, D.C.,
Carnegie Endowment for International Peace, 1934.

62. Vattel, op. cit., p. 165.

63. Only recently have some Western writers again
turned their attention to the concept of unequal treaties. This has probably been a result of the current
usage by the Communist States, especially the PRC. See

for example, I. Brownlie, Principles of Public International Law, London, Oxford University Press, 1966, pp. 495-496. It is noteworthy that an examination of the indexes of the following modern texts in international law yielded no reference to "unequal treaties:" William Bishop, International Law, 3rd ed., Boston, Little, Brown and Co., 1971; James L. Brierly, The Law of Nations, London, Oxford Press, 1936; Herbert Briggs, The Law of Nations, New York, F.S. Crofts, 1938; Wolfgang Friedmann, Oliver J. Lissitzyn and Richard Pugh, International Law, St. Paul, Minn., West, 1969; Noyes E. Leech, Covey T. Oliver and Joseph M. Sweeney, The International Legal System, Mineola, New York, Foundation Press, 1973; Georg Schwarzenberger, A Manual of International Law, 5th ed., New York, Praeger, 1967.

64. Chiu, op. cit., p. 60.

65. China Yearbook 1929-1930, p. 824. Also see Chinese Social and Political Science Review, Vol. XII, Supp. 1928, p. 47.

66. Stanley F. Wright, China's Struggle for Tariff Autonomy: 1843-1938, Shanghai, Kelly and Walsh Ltd., 1938, pp. 437-439 and passim.

67. Ibid., pp. 603, 633.

68. For a discussion of the final abrogation of these treaties including the conclusion of new treaties by the United States and the United Kingdom on January 11 , 1943 which abolished extraterritorial rights in China as well as other concessions gained previously by these countries see, Wesley R. Fishel, The End of Extraterritoriality in China, Berkeley, University of California Press, 1952, esp. pp. 214-215; For a complete study of the Nationalist Chinese concept of unequal treaties see, Tseng Yu-kao, The Termination of Unequal Treaties in International Law, Shanghai, The Commercial Press, 1933.

69. Kozhevnikov, op.cit., p. 248; emphasis added.

70. Ibid.

71. Wang Yao-t'ien, Kuo-chi mao-yi t'iao-yueh ho hsieh-ting, (International Trade Treaties and Agreements), Peking, T'sai-cheng ching-chi ch'u-pan she, 1958, p. 10; quoted in Chiu, op. cit., pp. 61-62; translation of other relevant portions of this work can be found in Cohen and Chiu, op. cit., pp. 1118-1120 and passim.

72. At least one scholar has attributed similar dual criteria to the Japanese concept of unequal treaties, using both inequality of States and substantive textual considerations. See L. Jerold Adams, Theory, Law and Policy of Contemporary Japanese Treaties, Dobbs Ferry, New York, Oceana, 1974.

73. ILM, op. cit., p. 698.

74. Ibid., p. 733.

75. Chiu, op. cit., pp. 62-63.

76. Ibid., p. 63.

77. Wang Yao-t'ien, op. cit., p. 31.

78. UNTS 278:41; denounced in JMJP, December 31, 1956.

79. UNTS 77:77; denounced in JMJP, November 29, 1966.

80. This treaty denounced in JMJP September 13, 1965.

81. UNTS 43:136; denounced in C.K. Cheng, "The Philippines: America's Show Window of Democracy in Asia?", Peking Review, February 5, 1965, p. 21.

82. UNTS 136:211; denounced in 1950-1952 Kuo-chi t'iao-yueh chi, (International Treaty Series), Peking, 1952, p. 395.

83. Denounced in NCNA commentary of October 21, 1968; English translation appears in "Diabolical Social-Imperialist Face of The Soviet Revisionist Renegade Clique," Peking Review, October 25, 1968, p. 8.

84. UNTS 480:43; denounced in JMJP, August 10, 1963.

85. This treaty denounced in JMJP, June 13, 1968; English translation appears in "A Nuclear Fraud Jointly Hatched by the United States and the Soviet Union," Peking Review, June 21, 1968, p. 5.

86. Ibid.

87. Chiu, op. cit., p. 68.

88. Ibid.

89. Lee, op. cit., p. 34; TYC 9:65.

90. TYC 9:63

91. TYC 12:64

92. TYC 12:122

93. TYC 11:19

94. Lee, op. cit., p. 36.

95. UNTS 14:137

96. SCMP 1512:58

97. TYC 9:44; English translation appears in Peking Review, February 2, 1960.

98. Chiu, op. cit., p. 64.

99. See supra Ch. II note 2.

100. The Sino-Russian border treaties in question were, The Treaty of Aigun, (1858); The Treaty of Peking, (1860); and the Treaty of Ili, (1881); For a discussion of these treaties see supra Ch. I pp. 22-23.

101. Denunciation of these treaties along with The Treaty of Nanking, (1842); The Treaty of T'ientsin, (1858); The Protocol of Lisbon, (1887); The Treaty of Shimonoseki, (1895); and the Convention for the extension of Hong Kong, (1898), appeared in JMJP, March 8, 1963, p. 1.

102. John Gittings, Survey of the Sino-Soviet Dispute 1963-1967, London, Oxford University Press, 1968, p. 158.

103. The Soviets refused to acknowledge these as unequal treaties, invoking the 1924 Agreement on the General Principles for the Settlement of the Questions between the Republic of China and the Soviet Union which indicated that all unequal treaties between China and Tsarist Russia were abrogated. On the other hand, some Soviet writers claimed that these treaties were only rectificatinns of earlier unequal treaties forced on Russia by Imperialist

China. e.g. The Treaties of Nertchinsk (1689) and
Kiakhta (1721). See supra Ch. 1 pp. 18-19. For fur-
ther Soviet views see Soviet statement in Pravda,
March 30, 1969. The English translation appears in
"Soviet Statement on Border Clashes Urges Negotiation,"
CDSP Vol. 21, No. 13, (April 16, 1969) pp. 4-5; Also
see Gittings, op. cit., passim.

104. See for example case studies in Scheinman
and Wilkinson, International Law and Political Crisis,
Boston, Little, Brown, 1968.

105. ILM, op. cit., p. 702.

106. Oliver J. Lissitzyn, "Treaties and Changed
Circumstances (Rebus Sic Stantibus)," American Journal
of International Law, Vol. 61, No. 4, (October,1967),
p. 895.

107. Friedmann, et. al., op. cit., p. 334.

CHAPTER IV

THE NATURE AND SCOPE OF PRC TREATIES

Definition and Classification of Treaties

Wang Yao-t'ien in his work on International Trade Treaties defines treaties as "documents which relate to the establishment, modification or termination of the sovereign rights and duties between two or more states."[1] Still another author, Wei Liang, defines a treaty as "an agreement between two or more states which must have received the unanimous consent of all contracting parties."[2]

Not only are these definitions far from complete but they also do not reflect the actual PRC doctrine and practice toward treaties. Taken at face value they appear to be similar in nature to any definition that one might find in a Western international law text. They do not, however, even allude to such important factors in PRC treaty theory and practice as equal and unequal treaties.[3] They are, nonetheless, probably the only formal definitions of treaties, as such, that exist by PRC writers.[4]

According to PRC theory only States may be parties to treaties. In PRC practice, however, we often find a divergence from theory. At times this divergence has apparently been motivated by ideological

reasons while at other times the motivation has been purely pragmatic. On the ideologically motivated side, PRC practice seems to indicate that revolutionary groups have the capacity to conclude treaties. There are several agreements and joint communiques included in the official treaty series (TYC) which have been concluded between the PRC and a revolutionary group.[5]

In July 1949 prior to the establishment of the PRC in October 1949, the Manchurian People's Government concluded a trade treaty with the Soviet Union. The PRC also issued several joint communiques with the Provisional Government of Algeria, which at the time existed only in Cairo and was something like a government in exile with a "reverse time lag"; i.e., exiled governments normally post-date regular governments but the Algerian one pre-dated its own existence as a national government.[6]

From a purely pragmatic point of view, the PRC has concluded a large number of semi-official agreements which take the form of treaties. These agreements often are concluded between a special agency in the PRC and a like agency in another country. Japan especially has concluded many agreements with the PRC in this fashion. That the PRC considers these arrangements as having the binding force of treaties there seems little doubt.[7] Moreover, they are inclu-

ded in the official TYC.[8]

It has increasingly become the practice in Western international law to treat international organizations as subjects of international law,[9] and their capacity to include treaties[10] is not the only proof, but probably the surest proof in both theory and practice. No such practice, let alone theory, has been followed by the PRC. According to PRC theory and practice international organizations do not possess an international personality comparable to that of States and therefore cannot become parties to treaties.[11]

Contrary to this interpretation Hungdah Chiu has cited two examples that seem to indicate that, "The practice of Communist China does not seem to exclude international organizations from concluding treaties."[12] The first example cited by Chiu is the PRC participation in the agreement establishing the International Organization for the Cooperation of Railroads which provides that the legal status of its employees in member States will be decided jointly by the organization and the State involved. Chiu states that, "Presumably, this could be decided through the conclusion of a separate treaty."[13] His second example is the Korean Armistice Agreement signed with the United Nations Command in Korea which is included in

the appendix to the TYC, (usually reserved for semi-
official agreements).

In my opinion these two examples are not enough
to support Chiu's interpretation. In the first case,
the treaty contains no stipulation as to the method
by which the legal status of employees will be determined, and it is much more likely in normal international organization practice that it will be done by
internal quasi-parliamentary means rather than by
treaty. Certainly past PRC practice would indicate
that this should be a more valid assumption. Even if
a treaty were used in that matter it is not unlikely
that the PRC would probably theorize that it made the
agreement with the other States rather than with the
organization,[14] and depending on procedural particu-
lars, this can be an arguable position even under
Western international law.

The second example is an armistice agreement and
hence by definition a non-routine matter that is not
well comparable with usual or regular treaty practices.
Thus in the particular case of treaties with international organizations it is reasonable to assert that
the PRC does in fact adhere to its own legal position,
and even if Chiu's examples were to be conceded as
valid exceptions they would still remain miniscule
exceptions to an overwhelmingly uniform practice.

Nomenclature of Treaties

Treaty is a generic term and refers to international contractual arrangements that may be called by any of many possible names, e.g. treaty, convention, agreement, protocol, etc. Western International Law does not treat these various names as having any theoretical significance. For example, Schwarzenberger states,

> Treaties, conventions, agreements, protocols, exchanges of notes or other synonyms all mean the same thing: consensual engagements under international law. All of these are governed by the same rules.[15]

The 1969 Vienna Convention also fails to mention any differences between terms, preferring to call them all treaties. In spite of the lack of any legal distinction, however, there is a sense of distinction in international practice as to the degree of formality and the various functions that each category of agreement is to perform. Unlike most Western international writers, PRC writer Wang Yao-ti'en has set forth an explanation for each of six names of treaties.

> (1) Treaty (t'iao-yueh)- This name is used to designate the most important of international documents, regulating the political, economic or other relations between contracting states, such as a treaty of alliance and mutual assistance or a treaty of commerce and navigation.

> (2) Agreement (hsieh-ting) - A treaty regulating special or provisional problems of the contracting states is called an "agree-

ment," such as a trade agreement or a payment
agreement.

(3) Convention   (kung-yueh or chuan-yueh)-
An agreement regulating special problems
among several states is called "convention"
(kung-yueh) such as a postal convention or
a telecommunication convention. A bilateral
agreement of this type is generally translated into Chinese as "chuan-yueh" (convention), such as a consular convention or a
boundary convention.

(4) Declaration   (hsuan-yen)- This is an
international document which generally provides only for general principles of international relations and international law.
Sometimes it also provides for specific obligations, such as the 1856 Paris Declaration concerning the law of sea warfare or
the Cairo Declaration of December 1; 1943.

(5) Protocol   (i-ting-shu)- This is an
international document containing an agreement on individual problems. Sometimes it
amends, interprets or supplements certain
provisions of a treaty, such as the general
conditions for the delivery of goods concluded by foreign trade ministries of socialist
states or the Soviet-Japanese protocol on
reciprocal application of most-favored-nation treatment concluded on October 19, 1956.

(6) Exchange of notes   (huan-wen)- These
are notes exchanged between two states to
define certain matters already agreed upon
by them. 16

In addition to the above cited terms the PRC also

has treaties called by the following names: Joint

Communique (lien-ho kung-pao), Joint Statement (lien-

ho sheng-ming or kung-t'ung sheng-ming), Joint Arrange-

ment (kung-t'ung pan-fa), Memorandum (pei-wang-lu),

Press Communique (hsin-wen kung-pao) and Contract

(ho-t'ung). Arrangements with the above titles are

sometimes included in the TYC and at other times are
not. The distinction for inclusion is not clear.[17]

The treaties included in the present study have
been categorized according to the categories used in
the Treaty Information Project.[18] All categories except the residual "other" group happen to correspond
to the official document title found on each PRC
treaty. The categories of the Treaty Project are (1)
Treaty, (2) Convention, (3) Agreement, (4) Exchange of Notes, (5) Protocol, and (6) Other. Only
those documents which appear to be original documents
were included in the present study. Subsequent arrangements which merely prolong or amend prior treaties were not included. This was done for the sake
of comparability with the UNTS where post-treaty documents are handled in the "Annex" rather than as separate treaties. Contracts, though not normally included in treaty studies, have been included under the
category "Other" due to their importance to the PRC's
international dealings.

Wang's qualitative assessment of the uses of the
different categories of treaties seems to be borne
out in quantitative terms as well. The PRC has definitely reserved the use of the term treaty (t'iao-
yueh) for special documents. There are only 31 treaties in all which bear the most formal title of

116

t'iao-yueh. All but two of these treaties fall into
the Diplomacy/Administration category. The two exceptions are both boundary treaties, one with Burma
and one with Afghanistan, and might well be called
"treaties" under similar circumstances in Western
practice too.

The term "agreement" (hsieh-ting) is the single
most frequently used title in PRC practice. Nearly
40% of all PRC treaties use this term. This is not
surprising since according to Wang this term is used
especially for trade and payments treaties, and that
is the largest topic category among PRC treaties.

The term "protocol" (i-ting-shu) is used in 29%
of the PRC's treaties. There is little reliance on
the form of treaty known as "exchange of notes or
letters" (huan-wen). Less than 6% are of this type.
Declarations, contracts, etc. have been categorized
under "other" and comprise the remaining 22% of the
treaties. There are no bilateral treaties which bear
the title of "convention" (chuan-yueh)[19], and there are
few in Western practice as this title is used primarily for multilateral arrangements.

Attempts were made to analyze the frequency of
use of various kinds of agreements with the various
country groupings. The resulting correlations, however, are probably spurious. For example, the Western

nations tended to rank highest in numbers of "agreements" (hsieh-ting) signed with the PRC, whereas the
Communist States ranked higher in less formal arrangements. However, rather than any country group variable causing this relationship it seems that topic
category is the more likely explanation. The Western
States deal with the PRC mostly in the area of trade
and it has already been stated that "agreements" are
the most frequently used treaty type for this topic.[20]

Topic Classification

The official Compilation of Treaties of the
People's Republic of China classifies treaties into
14 main topic categories. Five of these categories
are further subcategorized. The categories are as
follows:

1. Political
    (1) Friendship
    (2) Joint announcement, communique, or
         declaration
    (3) Others
2. Legal
    (1) Consular relations
    (2) Nationality
3. Boundary
4. Boundary problems (use of boundary river,
    etc.)
5. Economic
    (1) Commerce and navigation
    (2) Economic aid, loan, and technical
         cooperation
    (3) Trade and payment
    (4) General conditions for delivery of
         goods
    (5) Registration of trademark
    (6) Others

6.   Cultural
    (1) Cultural cooperation
    (2) Broadcasting and television cooperation
    (3) Exchange of students
    (4) Others
7.   Science and technology
8.   Agricultural and forest
9.   Fishery
10. Health and sanitation
11. Post and telecommunication
12. Communication and transportation
    (1) Railways
    (2) Air transportation
    (3) Water transportation
    (4) Highway
13. Law of war
14. Military[21]

These categories apply to offical treaty agreements between States. Other agreements such as those discussed above are accorded unofficial status and are included only in the appendix of the TYC.

In view of the fact that part of the objective of this study is to compare the PRC treaty practice both qualitatively and quantitatively with other States individually as well as with the world as a whole, and since the PRC categories are idiosyncratic it has been necessary to classify the PRC treaties into topic categories which make them comparable with the UNTS data base.

The classification of treaties into a limited number of topic categories is not an easy task. To facilitate categorization, the "one treaty, one topic" principle has been followed as developed in the

Treaty Information Project.[22] Treaties were placed
under the category with which the main theme of the
treaty was concerned. There are obvious limitations
to this method especially when desiring to closely define treaty topics. However, the ease of handling and
the gain in comparability far outweigh the disadvan-
tages. In order to prevent distortions among the
finely defined subcategories of the Treaty Information Project, this study is limited to the Project's
eight broad categories; i.e., (1) diplomacy and administration, (2) health, education and welfare, (3)
trade and payments, (4) aid and assistance, (5) transportation and communication, (6) military and occupation, (7) international organizations, and (8) ad hoc
matters.[23]

The topic "diplomacy and administration" includes
all treaties dealing with diplomatic, consular and
other administrative matters such as visas, frontier
formalities, status of refugees and general friendly
relations. Most of the treaties included in the first
four categories of the TYC treaty classification system, i.e., Political, Legal, Boundary and Boundary
problems, with their relative sub-categories, are included in this topic heading.

"Health, education and welfare" includes, inter-
alia, agreements on research and scientific projects,

cultural and educational exchanges as well as labor relations and humanitarian issues. TYC topics (6) Cultural, (7) Science and Technology and (10) Health and Sanitation are included in this topic heading.

"Trade and payments " covers the entire range of subjects included in the TYC topic heading "Economic" (5), with the exception of aid and loans, (TYC topic 5, subtopic 2). Those topics are covered in our general topic category called "aid and assistance." That topic category also includes technical assistance and aid and development missions.

"Transportation and communication" covers the TYC topic categories (11) Post and Telecommunication and (12) Communication and Transportation.

The topic category "military and occupation " is the equivalent of the TYC topic categories (13) Law of War and (14) Military.

Our topic (8) ad hoc matters refers to treaties which deal with the ad hoc disposition of particular issues such as the disposition of specific goods, equipment or territory. It also includes the treatment of specific resources and would therefore include TYC topic categories (8) Agriculture and forest and (9) Fishery.

There are no bilateral PRC treaties which come under the topic "international organizations." (For

a complete listing of the Treaty Information Project
topics and sub-topics see appendix table 1).

The Treaty Making Process

In practice the PRC seems for the most part, to
follow generally accepted norms and procedures for the
negotiation, conclusion, and ratification of international agreements. In view of the fact that the PRC
practice in these procedural matters does not differ
to any great degree from Western practice and in view
of the fact that the PRC's treaty making process has
been dealt with in detail by several other authors,[24]
the following discussion will briefly summarize a
broad overview of the PRC's practice. Only those
areas which seem to be at odds with accepted Western
practices will be discussed in detail.

Constitutional Provisions

According to the 1954 Constitution of the People's
Republic of China two organs of the government are
chiefly responsible for the carrying out of international relations and, ipso facto, for the negotiation
and conclusion of treaties. Article 31 of the PRC
Constitution states inter alia,

> The standing Committee of the National
> People's Congress exercises the following
> functions and powers:
>
> (11) To decide on the appointment or

recall of plenipotentiary representatives to foreign states;

(12)   To decide on the ratification
or abrogation of treaties concluded
with foreign states;[25]

In addition, the Standing Committee has the power to

decide on "the proclamation of war ... in fulfillment

of international treaty obligations concerning common

defense against aggression."[26]

Signature

The Chief of State or Chairman of the PRC is

the person directly responsible for the signing of

treaties and the appointment of the proper official

to act as plenipotentiary. The plenipotentiary may

be the Chairman himself, the foreign minister, the

premier, or any other designated official. As sta-

ted above, all appointments of plenipotentiaries are

subject to the approval of the Standing Committee.

Article 41 Section II of the Constitution regarding

the duties of the Chairman of the PRC reads as fol-

lows:

The Chairman of the People's Republic
of China represents the People's Republic
of China in its relations with foreign
states, receives foreign diplomatic representatives, and, in pursuance of decisions
of the Standing Committee of the National
People's Congress, appoints or recalls plenipotentiary representatives to foreign
states and ratifies treaties concluded
with foreign states.[27]

The PRC practice regarding signature follows Western practice. As has become the increasingly frequent practice of Western States the PRC concludes most of its agreements by signature alone. Nearly 85% of the agreements to which the PRC is party come into force by signature alone.[28] This compares with a world average of 63% for the period 1962-1965.[29]

In addition, evidence indicates that they also subscribe to the Western principle of signature ad referendum, whereby a signature ad referendum or mere "initialing" of a treaty does not create a binding obligation on the part of the signing or initialing government. This particular point was made very strongly by the PRC in relation to the Sino-Indian border dispute over the validity of the McMahon Line.[30] The PRC claims that the draft treaty of the 1914 Simla conference is not binding on China since the Chinese representative only initialed his name.[31]

Ratification

The power to ratify treaties is granted to the Standing Committee by Article 31 of the 1954 Constitution.[32] In practice the ratification procedure has differed significantly through three historical periods. Prior to the adoption of the 1954 Constitution the provisions for ratification were stipulated in the

Organic Law of the Central People's Government of the People's Republic adopted in 1949. Article 6 of the Organic Law grants the power to ratify, abrogate or revise treaties to the Central People's Government Council.

After 1954, agreements which must be ratified are first passed by the State Council, then submitted to the National People's Congress Standing Committee and finally formally acted upon by the Chairman of the PRC in pursuance of the decision of the Standing Committee. Other agreements which merely require approval are submitted only to the State Council. According to Hsiung, a more recent practice has been to obtain prior approval from the Standing Committee so that the PRC Chairman can conclude treaties that are effective on signing.[33] This is consistent with the PRC practice of concluding most of its agreements on the basis of signature alone.

As a result of the Great Proletarian Cultural Revolution (GPCR) the current ratification process is in doubt. No treaties requiring formal ratification have been concluded subsequent to the GPCR. However, the process of approval by the State Council still appears to be in effect. On March 14, 1967, at the height of the Cultural Revolution, the State Council granted approval to the Sino-Mauritanian Agreement

on Economic and Technical Cooperation.[34]

The types of treaties requiring ratification have been stipulated by a resolution passed by the Standing Committee on October 16, 1954. Article 1 of this resolution reads as follows:

> 1. The following types of treaties concluded by the People's Republic of China with foreign States will be ratified in accordance with the provisions of Article 31, Section 12, and Article 41 of the Constitution of the People's Republic of China: peace treaties; treaties of non-aggression; treaties of friendship, alliance and mutual assistance; and all other treaties, including agreements (hsieh-ting), which contain stipulations that they will be submitted for ratification.[35]

Article 2 of the same resolution states that all other treaties not included in the first article should be approved by the State Council.

Accession and Adherence

The PRC has acceded to a small number of multilateral conventions. The acceptance of the convention in practice is promulgated by a resolution of the NPC Standing Committee. The foreign ministry of the State Council then transmits the instrument of accession to the depository.[36] In view of the small number of multilateral conventions to which the PRC has acceded, little can be said in regard to their formal practice. In all but two cases, the PRC government has insisted on replacing the Nationalist

government as party to the treaty.[37]

Though PRC policy concerning reservations has not been clearly articulated, practice suggests that they follow the Soviet policy in claiming that a State has the sovereign right to make reservations to multilateral treaties without the consent of the other contracting parties.

Registration

Article 102 of the United Nations Charter requires that member States register their treaties with the Secretariat. Since the PRC has only recently become a member of the U.N. it is not surprising that only a few of its treaties are registered with the United Nations.[38] All PRC treaties thus far registered with the United Nations and which appear in the UNTS have been registered by the PRC's treaty partner. It is too early to tell exactly what the PRC practice will be toward registration. It has been noted in Chapter I that Western practice in this matter is far from consistent in spite of the Charter provisions.[39]

Effect of Treaties

It is generally accepted by most scholars of PRC legal practice that the PRC respects and adheres to the doctrine of *pacta sunt servanda*.[40] There are, however, some conditions to the strict adherence of

this principle. The primary requisite is that the treaty must be based on equality of parties, and on substantive equality of the treaty provisions. The treaty must create "equal and reciprocal" privileges and obligations or the treaty is considered to be unequal and therefore void ab initio [41]

The PRC also apparently adheres to the principle of pacta tertiis nec nocent nec prosunt. They have invoked this principle in relation to the binding nature of resolutions by the United Nations. They have informed the UN in the past that without representation in that body, "the Chinese people have no obligation to abide by the resolutions and decisions of the United Nations."[42]

The principle of pacta tertiis has also been invoked to denounce the British-Russian treaty concerning the status of Tibet. In commenting on the nature of the binding force of the agreement on China, Yu Fan wrote that the convention "was concluded only between Britain and Russia and can only be effective between Britain and Russia."[43] Yu Fan cites the principle of pacta tertiis as the basis for the claim that the agreement has created no obligation for China.

The PRC does not only use this principle to its own advantage. They have, in their own treaty mak-

ing, taken care so as not to abridge the rights of third States. For example, the PRC took care in the Sino-Pakistan Boundary Agreement of 1963 to include a clause stating that the terms of the agreement would not prejudice India's interests in the dispute between her and Pakistan over Kashmir.[44]

Most-Favored-Nation Clauses

One particular concept that is related, but does not run counter, to the principle of pacta tertiis is the principle of most-favored-nation treatment. Once a malevolence perpetrated against the Chinese Empire, threatening its destruction, the most-favored-nation clause has been utilized by the Chinese Communists to circumvent discriminatory policies by certain unfriendly governments which were aimed at weakening its internal and global positions.

During their "attack" on the Chinese Empire, the Western nations as well as Russia and Japan used the unilateral most-favored-nation clause to gain extreme privileges and concessions such as the granting of territory through lease arrangements and extra-territorial jurisdiction. These concessions, granted without reciprocity, aided in the eventual demise of the Chinese Empire. In addition, they

threatened to cause a division of China into colonial
entities. All treaties granting unilateral most-favored-nation clauses were abrogated and renegotiated
by the Nationalist Chinese about the time of the end
of World War II.

Because of the antagonistic posture toward the
Communist regime exhibited by the United States and
the trade embargo imposed on them by the United States
and many of its allies, the PRC found the most-favored-
nation clause to be a useful tool in insuring equal
treatment from those nations with which she was able
to trade. At least one PRC writer has hailed the
policy as a most effective way to combat these "discriminatory policies" in world trade.[45]

PRC writer Wang Yi-wang has defined the most-
favored-nation clause in the following manner:

> ...when one of the contracting parties
> grants certain favorable treatment to a
> third party, the other contracting party
> will automatically enjoy the same privi-
> lege.[46]

This is similar to Western definitions of the most-
favored-nation clause.[47] Moreover, the PRC, similar to
contemporary Western practice, uses the most-favored-
nation clause to apply only to commercial and economic
matters. The first instance of the use of the most-
favored-nation clause was in the Sino-Egyptian Trade
Agreement of August 22, 1955.[48] In this treaty both

countries agreed to grant most-favored-nation treatment in the issuance of import-export licenses and
customs duties. Subsequent treaties in many cases
have given wider application to the most-favored-
nation treatment.

The wording and scope of the most-favored-nation
clause is by no means the same in all treaties wherein it is found. For example, treaties with Communist
countries provide for most-favored-nation treatment
in many more issues than do the treaties with non-
Communist States. Two treaties signed within a short
time of each other will serve as an example.

The first treaty, the Sino-Ceylonese Agreement
on Trade and Payments concluded on September 19, 1957
calls for most-favored-nation treatment

> "in respect of the issue of import and
> export licenses, and the levy of cus-
> tom duties, taxes and any other charges
> imposed on or in connection with the
> importation, exportation and tranship-
> ment of commodities...[49]

On the other hand the Sino-Soviet Treaty of Commerce and Navigation concluded on April 23, 1958
calls for a much broader range of subjects to be included in the most-favored-nation treatment. Article
2 which outlines the general provisions of the most-
favored-nation treatment covers, "all matters relating to trade, navigation and other economic relations

between the two States."[50]

The most-favored-nation clause is included in many, but not all, of the trade treaties of the PRC. Countries excluded comprise both Communist and non-Communist nations; countries included are of a similar mixture. There is no clue to the system or rationale of selection. J.C. Hsiung suggests that the absence of most-favored-nation arrangements with certain countries reflects the nature of the relations existing with those countries and is not necessarily reflective of restraint of trade policies.[51] By 1968 the PRC had trade agreements of both official and semi-official nature with 48 States. Of those 48 States, 29 had most-favored-nation arrangements with the PRC.

Dispute Settlement and Arbitration

The PRC practice relating to the settlement of disputes arising over treaties differs considerably from that of most States. Many of the world's treaties (6%) now contain clauses which refer disputes arising over treaties to the International Court of Justice for settlement.[52] None of the PRC treaties contain such a provision.

The PRC stand on the question of dispute settlement by third parties is clear. They are against it,

and regard the settlement of disputes over treaties
to be the sole province of the contracting parties.
PRC writer Wang Yao-t'ien writes:

> Since the subjects of international
> treaties are sovereign states, there can-
> not be a supra-national organ in interna-
> tional affairs to interpret international
> treaties and compel the contracting par-
> ties to accept its interpretation. Conse-
> quently, the interpreters of international
> treaties can only be the contracting states
> themselves, and the best method of settling
> this problem is through diplomatic negoti-
> ation.[53]

Thus, the intervention in a dispute by a third party,
such as the ICJ, is regarded as an infringement upon
State sovereignty. This is true even though cases
can only be judged by the Court after agreement between the parties to submit the case to the Court
for judgement.[54] The PRC view that negotiations
serve as the best means of dispute settlement is
similar to that of the Soviet Union.[55]

Some of the PRC's treaties do provide arbitration clauses in the event that matters are unable to
be brought to a satisfactory conclusion by negotiation. Two primary PRC bodies govern the provisions
for arbitration. They are the Foreign Trade Arbitration Commission of the China Council for the Pro-
motion of International Trade and the Maritime Arbitration Commission of the same body.[56]

In those treaties containing arbitral clauses

the composition of the tribunal varies. In some agreements the arbitrators must be citizens of either country party to the treaty.[57] In others they must be solely
from the country in which the arbitration is to take
place.[58] In still others arbitrators may be selected
from "the nationals of a third country agreed upon by
both contracting parties."[59]

FOOTNOTES

1. Wang Yao-t'ien, Kuo-chi mao-yi t'iao-yueh ho hsieh-ting, (International Trade Treaties and Agreements) Peking, 1958, p. 9.

2. Wei Liang, "Looking at the So-Called McMahon Line from the Viewpoint of International Law," Kuo-chi wen-t'i yen-chiu, (Studies in International Problems) Peking, 1960, No. 6, p. 46.

3. For a discussion of unequal treaties see supra, Ch. III pp. 85-99.

4. Hungdah Chiu states that these are the only two authors known to him that have given definitions of treaties. He does suggest one other author who may have defined treaties. He is Kuo Chao in his "The Names and Kinds of International Treaties," Chi-lin jih-pao (Kirin Daily), April 4, 1957, p. 4. This source is apparently not available in this country. See Hungdah Chiu, The People's Republic of China and the Law of Treaties, Cambridge, Harvard University Press, 1972, p. 8.

5. See for example, TYC 7:9, Joint Communique issued during the visit to Peking by Mahmoud Cherif, member of the Algerian Provisional Government.

6. Ibid.

7. See Luke T. Lee, China and International Agreements, Durham, N.C., Rule of Law Press, 1969, pp. 69-85 and passim.

8. For a discussion of the inclusion of these semi-official documents in the TYC see infra, pp.113-115.

9. See, Reparations for Injuries Suffered in Service of The United Nations, International Court of Justice, Advisory Opinion, 1949, ICJ (1949) 174; cited in Wolfgang Friedmann, Oliver J. Lissitzyn and Richard C. Pugh, International Law, St. Paul, Minn., West, 1969, pp. 202-203.

10. Hungdah Chiu, The Capacity of International Organizations to Conclude Treaties and the Special Legal Aspects of the Treaties so Concluded, The Hague, Martinus Nijhoff, 1966.

11. See for example, K'ung Meng, "A Criticism of the Theories of Bourgeois International Law on Subjects of International Law and the Recognition of States," Kuo-chi wen-t'i yen-chiu, (Studies in International Problems) Peking, 1960, No. 2, pp. 50-51.

12. Chiu, supra, note 4, pp. 10-11.

13. Ibid., p. 10

14. For a discussion on this point see, James C. Hsiung, Law and Policy in China's Foreign Relations, New York, Columbia University Press, 1972, pp. 229-231.

15. Georg Schwarzenberger, A Manual of International Law, 5th ed., New York, Praeger, 1967, p. 151.

16. Wang Yao-t'ien, op. cit., p. 12; translated in Jerome A. Cohen and Hungdah Chiu, People's China and International Law: A Documentary Study, Princeton, Princeton University Press, 1974, p. 1163.

17. See supra, Ch. I.

18. Treaty Information Project, University of Washington, Professor Peter H. Rohn, Director. See list of various publications produced under Treaty Project auspices in supra Ch. I, note 13.

19. In normal international practice this category is usually reserved for multilateral agreements.

20. For a discussion of the correlation between treaty topics and titles see Juris A. Lejnieks, "The Nomenclature of Treaties; A Quantitative Analysis, The Texas International Law Forum, Vol. II, No. 2, Summer 1966, pp. 175-188.

21. This listing has been compiled from the TYC by Hungdah Chiu and can be found in Chiu, supra, note 4, pp. 21-22.

22. See Peter H. Rohn, supra, Ch. I, note 13.

23. For a complete listing of all subtopics included in the general categories see Appendix Table I.

24. See supra, Ch. I, note 30.

25. Constitution of the People's Republic of

China, Adopted by the First National People's Congress of the People's Republic of China, September 20, 1954, Peking, Foreign Languages Press, 1954, pp. 23-24.

26. Ibid., p. 24.

27. Ibid., p. 28.

28. See table in Chiu, supra, note 4, pp. 38-41.

29. Curtis G. Reithel, "A Quantitative Analysis of Treaties Entering into Force Upon Signature," Treaty Information Project working paper #36, University of Washington, October, 1970, p. 6.

30. The McMahon Line was established as part of the border between China and India by the 1914 Simla Conference.

31. For a discussion of the Chinese viewpoint on the validity of the Simla Conference see Chiu, supra, note 4, p. 34 and Hsiung, op. cit., pp. 237-238.

32. Constitution, op. cit., p. 24.

33. Hsiung, op. cit., p. 238.

34. SCMP 3907:38

35. Chung-hua jen-min kung-ho kuo fa-kuei hui-pien, (Collection of Laws and Regulations of the People's Republic of China) Vol. I, p. 207.

36. Hsiung, op. cit., p. 239.

37. See supra, note 7.

38. It is worth noting that at least one non-member registers its treaties with the U.N., i.e., Switzerland as of 1973.

39. See supra, Ch. I, pp. 9-10 .

40. See for example, Lee, op. cit., passim.

41. See supra, note 3.

42. "Speech by Wu Hsiu-ch'uan, "Current Background, U.S. Consulate, Hong Kong, No. 36, 1950.

43. Yu Fan, "Speaking of the Relationship be-

tween China and the Tibetan Region from the viewpoint of Sovereignty and Suzerainty," JMJP, June 5, 1959.

44.   There were actually two boundary documents. An Agreement on March 2, 1963, TYC 12:64 and a Joint Communique, TYC 12:1; Article 6 of the Agreement is the provision for the protection of the rights of India in the border settlement.

45.   Wang Yao-t'ien, op. cit., pp. 28, 134.

46.   Wang Yi-wang, "What is the difference between Commercial Treaties and Trade Treaties," Kwangming jih-pao, (Enlightenment Daily) May 12, 1950, p.3.

47.   See for example, Schwarzenberger, op. cit., p. 110.

48.   TYC 4:123; The English text appears in SCMP 1151:64

49.   TYC 6:203; UNTS 337:139

50.   TYC 7:42; UNTS 313:135

51.   Hsiung, op. cit., p. 267.

52.   Peter H. Rohn, Treaty Profiles, Santa Barbara, Calif., American Bibliographical Center, Clio Press, 1975.

53.   Wang Yao-t'ien, op. cit., p. 14.

54.   The agreement does not have to be ad hoc but can be the result of a dispute settlement clause in a treaty or by prior acceptance, by both parties to the dispute, of the so called optional clause (Art. 36) of the Statute of the International Court of Justice.

55.   See for example, F.I. Kozhevnikov, ed., International Law, Moscow, Foreign Languages Publishing House, n.d., pp. 378-379; The Soviet Union has never included a clause referring settlement of disputes to the ICJ in any of its bilateral treaties, see Peter H. Rohn, "A Computer Search in Soviet Treaties, International Lawyer, Vol. 2, No. 4, (July, 1968) pp. 661-680.

56.   Lee, op. cit., pp. 215-223.

57. The Sino-Finnish Trade Agreement, June 5, 1953, <u>TYC</u> 2:37.

58. The Semi-Official Trade Agreement between China Import and Export Corporation and the French Industrial and Commercial Trade Delegation, June 5, 1953, <u>TYC</u> 2:37.

59. The Sino-Japanese Semi-Official Trade Agreement, March 5, 1958, <u>TYC</u> 7:197.

CHAPTER V

TREATY TRENDS AND PATTERNS

I shall now turn from the more traditional forms
of treaty analysis discussed above to the consideration of treaties as a quantifiable data base which can
be used as an indicator of the PRC's actions and intentions in the international system. Although, as
the preceding discussion has shown, there are often
significant differences between PRC theory and practice with regard to treaties, the differences tend
toward the normative in practice (i.e. toward those
norms prescribed by Western international law) and
the radical in theory. In other words, the PRC tends
to exhibit revolutionary tendencies when talking
about international law in general and treaties specifically, but tends to perform in those areas more as
a status quo oriented actor.

The implications are clear, then, for the reliability of our data base. The PRC's treaty practices
conform, to a significant degree, to the treaty prac-
tics of Western states and they are no less serious
about the obligations incurred as a result of their
treaty commitments. The treaties of the PRC should
provide a reliable data base for meaningful quantitative analysis of PRC international behavior.

139

It has been shown above that there has been an increasing reliance on treaties both as a source and substance of international law. Treaty volume has grown steadily since World War II, providing us with a global treaty data base of considerable magnitude. Since quantitative data is available on treaty trends and patterns for the PRC as well as for the rest of the world, we have the opportunity to add yet another indicator to the overall analysis of PRC international behavior, especially in comparison with other States singly and the world as a whole.

Overall Bilateral Treaty Frequency

There are 1,660 treaties included in this study covering a period of some 24 years, from late 1949 through October, 1972. During this period the PRC has entered into bilateral treaty arrangements with 79 States and other independent or semi-autonomous entities.[1] This results in an arithmetic mean of 21.01 treaties per partner. The distribution is skewed in favor of a few high frequency partners. The median score for all treaty partners is 7. Only 22 of the total 79 partners have treaty volumes in excess of the mean score of 21.01. Table 2 indicates treaty volume for all partners for the total period of the study.

Table 3 indicates total treaty volume for each year included in the study. There is a rather steady

increase in treaty volume for the entire span, peaking
in the 1964-65 period (240 treaties). Some small drop
can be noted in the 1958-59 period. This may in part
be attributed to the intensity with which the government devoted its energies to internal affairs during
the period of the Great Leap Forward.[2] A glance at
Table 1 (p. 12) indicating the Johnston and Chiu Calendar treaty listing which includes a broader range of
documents than are included in this data base, will
show that there was even a sharper decline in informal
documents during the 1958-59 period. This decline in
percent of less formal arrangements to formal documents may indicate a strongly felt need for external
security during a period of internal turmoil.

Chinese treaty frequency reached its highest
level in 1964 with a total of 127 treaties. During
the three-year period 1964-66, China entered into 328
bilateral agreements. After 1965, coincident with the
beginning of the Great Proletarian Cultural Revolution,
treaty volume declined sharply. As Morton Halperin
suggested in 1965, China certainly began "turning in"
during this period.[3] During the next three years,
at the height of the Cultural Revolution, China concluded only 108 treaties. The lowest volume year was
1969 with only 26 agreements.

TABLE 2

PRC TREATY PARTNERS
1949 - 1972

Rank	Country	Treaties	Rank	Country	Treaties
1.	USSR	141	41.	Morocco	7
2.	N. Vietnam	121	42.	S. Yemen	5
3.	N. Korea	117	43.	W. Germany	5
4.	Albania	91	44.	Laos	5
5.	Poland	78	45.	C. Africa	4
6.	Romania	74	46.	Denmark	4
7.	E. Germany	73	47.	Italy	4
8.	Czechoslovakia	73	48.	Norway	4
9.	Hungary	63	49.	U.K.	4
10.	Mongolia	62	50.	Kenya	4
11.	Ceylon	60	51.	Tunisia	4
12.	Bulgaria	57	52.	Lebanon	3
13.	Cuba	40	53.	Guyana	3
14.	Guinea	38	54.	Sweden	3
15.	Nepal	37	55.	Ethiopia	3
16.	Burma	35	56.	Rwanda	3
17.	Pakistan	34	57.	Burundi	3
18.	Finland	30	58.	Uganda	2
19.	Yugoslavia	29	59.	Camaroon	2
20.	Indonesia	26	60.	Eq. Guinea	2
21.	Mali	25	61.	Netherlands	2
22.	UAR	23	62.	Peru	2
23.	Afghanistan	19	63.	Switzerland	2
24.	Ghana	17	64.	Austria	2
25.	Syria	17	65.	Malagasy	1
26.	Cambodia	17	66.	Mauritius	1
27.	Tanzania	16	67.	Sierra Leone	1
28.	India	16	68.	Tanganyika	1
29.	Congo(Brazza.)	15	69.	Togo	1
30.	Iraq	15	70.	Hong Kong	1
31.	Japan	15	71.	Tibet	1
32.	Algeria	14	72.	Belgium	1
33.	Yemen (Sana)	13	73.	Brazil	1
34.	Sudan	12	74.	Canada	1
35.	Egypt	12	75.	Malta	1
36.	Somalia	9	76.	Mexico	1
37.	Zambia	8	77.	Portugal	1
38.	Chile	7	78.	Uruguay	1
39.	France	7	79.	United States	1
40.	Mauritania	7			

TABLE 3
TOTAL PRC TREATY VOLUME PER YEAR

Year	Treaty Volume
1949	3
1950	23
1951	24
1952	38
1953	44
1954	79
1955	85
1956	95
1957	88
1958	85
1959	90
1960	91
1961	109
1962	87
1963	100
1964	127
1965	113
1966	88
1967	44
1968	38
1969	26
1970	54
1971	69
1972*	60
Total	1,660

*1972 is complete only through October

In 1971, Daniel Tretiak asserted that China had
again begun to "turn out."[4] Tretiak analyzed levels
of international news contained in the Peking Review
for the period 1966-1969 to support this contention.
His findings indicate that during the period from January 1966 to December 1969 the Peking Review devoted
an average of 50.29% of its coverage to international
news, a significant amount by any standards.[5] Chinese
treaty patterns for the period 1970-72 lend additional
evidence to Tretiak's argument. During this period
each year showed an increase in volume over the previous year.

Treaty Frequency by Country Groupings

Table 4 indicates bilateral treaty frequency for
2-year periods by country group partners of the PRC.
For purposes of comparison I have categorized China's
treaty partners into six country groupings: (1) Soviet-
Core-Bloc-includes those East European Communist States
that have maintained strong political and economic
ties with the Soviet Union, and includes the U.S.S.R
itself; (2) PRC-Bloc-includes those communist nations
which have tended recently to move in a direction
away from strong Soviet domination and/or toward a
greater influence from China,i.e. Albania, N. Vietnam and N. Korea; (3) Asia - includes all non-communist

Asian countries plus Mongolia; (4) Arab - includes all
Arab States; (5) Africa - includes all sub-Saharan
African States; (6) Western Nations - includes all
nations with a Western "Free World" political orienta-
tion and which are not included in one of the other
groups.[6] Yugoslavia and Cuba, due to their special
relationships with both of the major Communist powers
have been treated separately.

Since absolute treaty values make meaningful comparison over time difficult, treaty volume for each
country group has been calculated in percent per two-
year period. Biennial periods have been chosen for
comparison in order to eliminate much of the distortion that might arise from year to year fluctuations.
Perusal of the resulting data has indicated that this
yields more reliable statistics for the analysis of
trends and patterns over time.

The most productive method of comparison is to
compare the percentage of the total number of treaties
concluded for several sample periods by each country
grouping. Six periods of two years will be used for
this comparison: 1954-55, 1958-59, 1962-63, 1964-65,
the period of decline 1966-67, and the period of re-
vitalization 1970-71. The 1954-55 period has been
chosen as the initial period for two reasons: (1)
prior to this period the influence from the Soviet

TABLE 4

PRC BILATERAL TREATY FREQUENCY

Country Groups *

Treaties per two-year period

	50-51	52-53	54-55	56-57	58-59	60-61	62-63	64-65	66-67	68-69	70-71
Sov-Core Bloc	43	46	70	74	85	63	54	51	30	11	23
PRC Bloc	1	3	42	35	37	40	38	44	28	12	38
Asia	3	17	32	31	23	48	37	51	27	12	18
Africa	0	0	0	1	2	17	22	52	27	22	18
Arab	0	0	10	10	17	10	14	23	8	4	11
West	0	16	10	16	7	6	11	10	8	1	10

*Yugoslavia and Cuba are not included

Union and the number of treaties accounted for by
them alone serve to distort the importance of the
comparisons; (2) 1954-55 is the first period in which
treaty volume in absolute numbers approaches what we
might see as a "norm" for the entire time span under
study.

The 1958-59 period has been chosen for three
reasons: (1) Prior to this period all country groupings showed a fairly steady increase in treaty frequency; (2) This is the period of greatest Soviet-
Core Bloc influence on the treaty totals; (3) This
is the period which included the decline presumably
caused by the failure of the Great Leap Forward.

The 1962-63 period is included because it is representative of the changes in treaty patterns caused
by the reawakening of the Sino-Soviet border dispute and shows important changes in bloc alignments
in PRC treaty volume.

The 1964-65 period is included because it includes the rapid growth in PRC treaty volume accounted
for by the African country group. It is also the
period of highest treaty making by the PRC (240 treaties). An additional reason for the inclusion of the
1962-63 and 1964-65 periods is that they represent,
in terms of overall volume, a kind of norm between
the Great Leap Forward period and the Great Prole-

tarian Cultural Revolution.

The 1966-67 period and the 1970-71 period have
been used since they represent the period of decline
in treaty volume brought about by the Cultural Revolution and the period of post-Cultural Revolutionary
recovery respectively. The 1968-69 period, which is
the nadir in PRC treaty volume has been omitted from
comparison as it was felt that the extremely low
volume would distort the percentage comparisons
among country groupings.

Table 5 indicates treaty frequency by percent
per biennial period. During the 1954-55 period the
Soviet-Core Bloc accounted for 43% of all PRC treaties. In the two previous two-year periods this country grouping had accounted for a much higher percentage of total PRC treaties. However, PRC treaty volume was extremely low from 1949 through 1953 and thus
the 1954-55 period is more representative of PRC
treaty patterns than prior periods during which the
PRC was attempting to stabilize itself after the
revolution. The PRC bloc countries accounted for
26% of PRC treaty volume during this period. The
only other significant country group was Asia with
20%. It is of some interest that, in spite of Soviet domination in PRC foreign affairs in this pre-
Great Leap period, Asia and the PRC bloc countries

accounted for 3% more of the PRC's treaties than the
Soviet-core bloc group. This is perhaps indicative
of the importance that the PRC attached to its geographic sphere of influence even at a very early
point in their existence. It is also perhaps a reit-
eration of China's historical concern with the general
Asian area.

During the 1958-59 period the Soviet Union and
Core Bloc States accounted for nearly 50% of all PRC
treaties. It is interesting to note that although
the total treaty frequency declined from the previous
2-year period (183 to 175), the Soviet-Core Bloc
treaties increased (74 to 85), (See table 4). This
represents a 9% gain over the previous 2-year span
in the proportion of treaties accounted for by the
Soviet-Core Bloc. It is apparent that Soviet dissatisfaction with the PRC over the Great Leap Forward
had not yet manifested itself in a decline in treaty
frequency between them. Since the failure of the
Great Leap was not yet apparent in 1958-59 and since
treaties tend to be retrospective indicators in cases
of this kind, i.e. where internal events lead to external occurrences, we would be more likely to see
the effects of the Great Leap Forward reflected in
later periods. The PRC Bloc countries Albania, North
Korea and North Vietnam accounted for over 20% of the

TABLE 5

PRC BILATERAL TREATY FREQUENCY

Country Groups*
% per two-year period

	50-51	52-53	54-55	56-57	58-59	60-61	62-63	64-65	66-67	68-69	70-71
Sov-Core Bloc	91	56	43	40	49	32	29	21	23	17	19
PRC Bloc	2	4	26	19	21	20	20	18	21	19	31
Asia	6	21	20	17	13	24	20	21	20	19	15
Africa	0	0	0	1	1	9	12	22	20	34	15
Arab	0	0	6	5	10	5	7	10	6	6	9
West	0	20	6	9	4	3	6	4	6	2	8

All figures in the chart above are percentages of total treaties for each two year period. The percentages have been rounded to the nearest whole percent and will therefore not total 100. *Yugoslavia and Cuba are not included.

treaties in the 1958-59 period. The Asian countries
accounted for approximately 13% and Africa only 1%.

The 1962-63 period begins to show a significant
change in bloc relationships with the PRC. The Soviet-Core Bloc in this period only accounted for
29% of the total treaties compared with 49% in the
1958-59 period. In absolute numbers this represents
a decrease of 32 treaties from the 1958-59 period
(from 85 to 54) and is a 37% decrease in Soviet-Core
Bloc-PRC treaty frequency in only five years. This
was the period of reawakening of the Sino-Soviet border dispute and other Chinese and Soviet disenchantment marked by the closing of two Soviet consulates in
Sinkiang at Urumchi and Kuldja in July of 1962.[7] It
seems evident that the Sino-Soviet dispute had a significant spillover effect on the other Core-Bloc
countries. Of the 31 treaty decrease, 21 were accounted for by the Core-Bloc and 11 by the Soviet
Union itself. Thus over 65% of the decrease was
accounted for by Core-Bloc countries other than the
U.S.S.R. On the other hand this period showed a significant rise in percentage of total treaties by the
Asian countries from 13% to 20%. Also showing a
great increase were the African countries from 1%

to 12%. Remaining constant were the PRC Bloc, still strong with 20%, and the Arab countries still relatively low with less than 7%.

The 1964-65 period again showed a decrease for the Soviet-Core Bloc from 29% to 21%. The most dramatic change during this period came from the African countries as they nearly doubled their percentage of total treaties from 12% to 22%. All other country groupings remained constant within 3% of the previous period.

The rapid increase in PRC-African treaty volume during this period is not altogether surprising since many of the States in this group had achieved their independence during, or just prior to, this time. Thus, part of the increase is attributable merely to the emergence of new States within the group. World treaty patterns also significantly reflect the emergence of newly formed African States. For example, in the 15 year period from 1946 through 1960, the African group of States accounted for only 2.8% of the world's treaty total, but in the subsequent five year period, from 1961 through 1965, this group contributed 18.7% of the world's total treaties. The great increase in treaty productivity of the African group over the entire 20 year span is dramatically illustrated by the fact that 72% of the African treaty total is accounted for in the last five years of the period.[8]

The rapid rise in African-PRC treaties cannot, however, be discounted entirely as being merely due to a rapid proliferation of States within the group. In comparative terms, the African group showed a greater percentage increase in PRC treaty totals than in world treaty totals. Further, the increase was more dramatic in that it took place over a shorter time span. Further support for the political significance of the increase in PRC-African treaties can be found in the 1968-69 period. During this period-- at the height of the Cultural Revolution--all country groups showed a decrease in both percent of total PRC treaties and in absolute number of treaties concluded except the African group which showed a percentage increase of 14% over the previous two-year period and only a slight decrease in absolute numbers from 27 in 1966-67 to 22 in 1968-69. It is evident then that there is strong PRC interest in Africa, even to the extent that it did not allow the Cultural Revolution to adversely affect their relations with that group of States. Evidence of the success of China's activities in Africa is that by 1965 half of Africa's independent States had recognized the PRC.

During the 1966-67 period all blocs and country groupings held constant within 4% of the previous two year period. In these last two periods it is signi-

ficant to note that 80% of China's treaties are now accounted for by 4 country groupings: Soviet-Core Bloc, PRC Bloc, Third World Asia and Africa, with an almost equal distribution among the four. It can be seen from the comparison that the PRC has increasingly, since the Sino-Soviet disenchantment, sought to broaden its treaty horizons away from the Soviet Union and toward the developing nations.

Several things are significant about the 1970-71 period. During this most recent period the Western nations accounted for their highest percentage (8%) of China's treaties since 1956-57. This represents an increase of 6% over the previous two-year period of PRC treaties accounted for by Western States. This is undoubtedly indicative of the increasingly friendly attitude that has been apparent between China and the West, particularly exemplified by the first visit of a U.S. President to the mainland of China. The PRC bloc countries during this period accounted for 31% of China's treaties, by far their highest total. This is not particularly surprising since these three countries have been extremely important to China in establishing its own political sphere of influence and it might be expected that during a period of increasing disenchantment between the two communist super powers the PRC would make

even greater efforts at further solidifying these already positive relationships.

Most notable in the 1970-71 period is an increase
in treaty frequency between China and the Soviet-
Core Bloc countries. This country group showed an
increase of 2% from the preceding two year period.
They accounted for 17% of all PRC treaties in 1968-69
and 19% in 1970-71. This certainly seems surprising
when one considers the continued, if not exacerbated,
Sino-Soviet rift and the obvious spillover effect that
it has had in past periods on treaty relations with
all of these countries. The explanation for this un-
expected increase lies with the tremendous rise in
treaty volume between the PRC and Romania. The entire
increase in this period is accounted for by Romania
which had 11 of the 23 treaties concluded between the
PRC and the Soviet-Core Bloc. Romania, which concluded only one treaty with the PRC in the 1968-69 period
concluded four treaties in 1970 and seven in 1971.
This is evidently a trend since they also concluded
three treaties with the PRC within the first few
months of 1972. By comparison the Soviet Union concluded only one treaty per year with the PRC in 1970,
71 and 72. Without the Romanian treaties, the Soviet-
Core Bloc would have continued to decline in treaty
frequency as expected.

The tremendous increase in Sino-Romanian treaty
activity plus recent Romanian actions vis-a-vis the
Soviet Union and China indicate they are growing
steadily away from the Soviet sphere of influence
and perhaps closer to China. In any event, treaty
analysis by country groupings in the future would have
to seriously consider Romania as excluded from the
Soviet-Core Bloc, perhaps having an independent status
equivalent to Cuba and Yugoslavia.

Treaty Frequency by Single Partners

In addition to treaty patterns by country groups
it is also important to look at treaty patterns across
a range of single partners. Certain shifts in the
PRC treaty patterns with individual States are infor-
mative in tracing the PRC's realignment in world politics and its emergence as a world power. Table 2
identifies the PRC's leading treaty partners for the
entire span of the study from 1949 through October
1972.

Of the 20 leading treaty partners, 13 can be
identified as Communist States. Of those 13 States,
three are geographically located in Asia. The remaining
States in the top 20 consist of five non-Communist
Asian States, one African and one Western State.
We find then, an ideological and geographic distribution of leading treaty partners that is particularly

indicative of the PRC's stance in world affairs, i.e.,
a newly-emerging State with a strong ideological doctrine which views itself as a significant force in
world politics but which nonetheless must come to
grips with the exigencies of Realpolitik, as all
States must, if they are to survive. Chinese foreign policy has been an attempt at combining ideologically motivated activities with international political pragmatism.[9] It will be shown below that there
is a significant change in rankings of the PRC's top
twenty partners over the last ten years of the study,
indicating that PRC needs and priorities have changed
considerably over time.

The top 10 ranking treaty partners for the entire period consist solely of countries which have
been identified as Core and PRC Bloc Communist countries. If we examine the PRC's 20 leading partners
for the past 10 years there are some interesting
changes in the rankings (See Table 6). The Soviet
Union, which is the PRC's leading treaty partner for
the entire period, has dropped below the top 10 for
the period 1963-72. In fact, all Soviet-Core Bloc
countries, with the exception of Romania have dropped
in ranking. Romania has increased its rank from 6th
to 4th in the last 10 year period.

Considering the entire 24 year period of the

study, the Soviet Union is still China's leading
over-all treaty partner with 141 agreements. This is
20 higher than North Vietnam, the next ranking partner
of the PRC. This total figure can be misleading, however, since in recent years a trend analysis shows
quite a different picture. Table 7 indicates that
the U.S.S.R. was the leading treaty partner with China
until 1962 when she lost that position and has never
regained it to the present. PRC-Soviet treaty frequency has continued to decline over the past ten
years. North Vietnam and North Korea have become the
PRC's leading partners since 1962 with a total of 53
and 46 treaties respectively for the period 1963-72,
compared with only 20 for the Soviet Union. Albania
has also become one of the PRC's leading treaty partners with a total of 91 treaties, ranking it fourth
overall. The 47 signed within the 1963-72 period make
Albania the PRC's second ranking treaty partner
during the last ten year period.

As noted previously, China obviously considers
these three States very important in its struggle
with the Soviet Union for preeminence among the
Communist States. Korea and Vietnam have, of course,
been significant to China since the times of "tributary States." The increasingly strong relationship
with Albania, however, represents a clear political

TABLE 6
PRC's 20 LEADING
TREATY PARTNERS
(1963 - 1972)

Rank	Country	Treaty Volume
1.	North Vietnam	53
2.	Albania	47
3.	North Korea	46
4.	Romania	34
5.	Ceylon	30
6.	Pakistan	28
7.	Guinea	27
8.	Nepal	23
9.	Cuba	21
10.	East Germany	21
11.	Poland	21
12.	Bulgaria	20
13.	Czechoslovakia	20
14.	USSR	20
15.	Mongolia	18
16.	Mali	18
17.	Hungary	17
18.	Tanzania	16
19.	Afghanistan	15
20.	Congo (Brazzaville)	15

TABLE 7

BILATERAL TREATY TRENDS 1949-1972
(two year periods)
For PRC's Three Leading Treaty Partners

	1949-50	1951-52	1953-54	1955-56	1957-58	1959-60
USSR	19	12	17	17	20	18
Korea (N.)	4	0	10	10	21	13
Vietnam (N.)	0	1	11	16	11	16

	1961-62	1963-64	1965-66	1967-68	1969-70	1971-72*	TOTALS
USSR	18	8	8	1	1	2	141
Korea (N.)	13	14	13	3	5	11	117
Vietnam (N.)	13	12	15	7	11	8	121

* 1972 is complete only through October

victory for the PRC and in view of the lack of any
historically significant ties between the PRC and
Albania, is probably a more definitive indicator of
the PRC's intentions toward what has traditionally
been regarded as "the Soviet Bloc." PRC-Albanian
treaties accurately reflect this relationship. From
the end of World War II Albania had been clearly and
strongly pro-Stalinist and definitely within the Soviet camp. Their constitution, adopted in 1946, under
the leadership of General Enver Hoxha, was modeled
on the Soviet Constitution. The Soviet Union pushed
strongly for the admission of Albania to the United
Nations in 1955 and that same year Albania was admitted to the Warsaw Pact. The first treaties between
the PRC and Albania were concluded in 1954. There
were six treaties concluded in that year on the general categories of cultural, economic and technical
cooperation. Perhaps most significant was a treaty
reportedly granting economic aid in the form of a
gift of ten million rubles to Albania.[10] From 1955
through 1960 Sino-Albania relations were good but were
maintained on a relatively low profile. The average
treaty frequency for the period was slightly less than
four treaties per year. In 1961 and 1962 the PRC concluded seven and eight treaties respectively with
Albania. This sudden rise in treaty volume was coin-

cident with the severing of Soviet-Albanian relations in December, 1961 and the barring of Albania from the Warsaw Pact meetings by the U.S.S.R. in 1962. In 1968, following the invasion of Czechoslovakia by the Soviets, Albania withdrew from the Warsaw Pact. PRC-Albanian treaty frequency continued high through 1968 averaging nearly six per year. In 1969, the year most affected by the Cultural Revolution, there were no treaties concluded with Albania, but in 1970 the PRC concluded eight treaties with Albania, primarily on the topics of trade and economic assistance.

The value of Albania to the PRC in the Sino-Soviet "propaganda war" is reflected in two separate editorials from the People's Daily. Following Albania's withdrawal from the Warsaw Pact a People's Daily editorial stated that "the Chinese people wholeheartedly support this revolutionary action by the Albanian people," since the Pact had become "an instrument for aggression in the hands of the Soviet revisionist renegade clique."[11]

An earlier editorial attacking the Soviet Communist Party also mentioned Albania.

> The leaders of the CPSU have openly called for the overthrow of the party and government leaders of Albania, brashly severed all economic and diplomatic relations with her, and tyranically deprived her of her legitimate rights as a member of the Warsaw Treaty Organization and the Council of Economic Mutual Assistance[12].

PRC actions, statements and treaty activity all clearly
indicate that Albania is now firmly in the Chinese
camp.

The spillover effect of the Sino-Soviet dispute on
the other Core-Bloc countries, as noted earlier, can
be easily seen when examining each country separately.
Prior to 1960 it was quite common for any one of these
countries to conclude 6 or 7 treaties per year with
the PRC. The total reached as high as 8 per year on
several occasions. Since 1960, however, the average
annual treaty frequency for these countries is 3 each.
The single exception is Poland whose annual average is
4. With the exception of Poland with 6 treaties in
1960 and Romania with 7 in 1971 no country has exceeded
5 in any one year since the Sino-Soviet split.

As noted earlier, Romania has become a significant
treaty partner of the PRC. The 34 Sino-Romanian
treaties concluded from 1963 through 1972 make Romania
the PRC's fourth ranking treaty partner for that ten-
year period. The peak year in the period was 1971
in which seven treaties were concluded, all on the
topics of trade and aid. Four of the seven treaties
were concerned with technical assistance, direct aid,
loans and credit. The PRC, however, has not had the
success with Romania that it has enjoyed with Albania.
It is apparent that Romania is willing to take what

China has to offer but is unwilling to ally herself
with the PRC against the Soviet Union. The visit to
Romania by U.S. President Richard Nixon in 1969 and
the return visits to the United States in 1970 and
1973 by Romanian President Nicolae Ceausescu coupled
with expanded treaty relations with China and
Ceausescu's 1974 announcement that the Soviets were
Romania's chief ally serve to indicate that Romania
intends to distribute its "eggs" carefully among the
competing super powers.

Cuba was at one time on her way to becoming one
of the PRC's leading treaty partners but during the
1965-67 period, her average annual treaty frequency
declined to 2 from an annual average of almost 6 for
the period 1960-64. The treaty patterns coincided
directly with the vigorous support given Cuba by
China, especially from the time of the Cuban missile
crisis in October 1962, followed by the growing disenchantment between Peking and Havana late in 1965,
prompted by the rice-sugar trade difficulties and
Cuba's apparent "Pro-Moscow course."[13]   Treaty frequency did increase to 3 in 1971, but only one treaty
had been signed through October of 1972.

In Asia, Mongolia is China's leading treaty partner with a total of 62 treaties. Although Mongolia
appears politically to be a great deal more in the

Soviet camp than the Chinese camp, the treaty frequency for Mongolia did not decline at all for several years after the Sino-Soviet split in 1960.
Outer Mongolian Premier Tsendenbal was very careful
to make it quite clear in December of 1962 that although he was in Peking to sign a border treaty, Mongolia was not abandoning her support of the Soviet
Union in the Sino-Soviet dispute.[14]   A New York Times
article noted that ,

> In the spring of 1964 it was reported that
> Security measures had been tightened along
> the Sino-Mongolian border and that Outer
> Mongolia was expelling all Chinese techni-
> cians and workers, allegedly in fear of a
> coup. [15]

Nonetheless treaty frequency between the PRC and
Mongolia remained at a reasonably high and constant
rate through 1966. It is rather difficult to explain
this constancy in treaty frequency in light of Mongolia's position and in light of the definite effect
that the Sino-Soviet dispute has had on the Core-Bloc
countries. Several possibilities suggest themselves.
The first, simplest and most obvious explanation is
mere geography. It is typical that States tend to
conclude more treaties with contiguous States, all
other things being equal. Of course one could reasonably assert that Mongolia's location between the two
competing communist super powers does not make "other

things equal." A second explanation is that perhaps
Mongolia was attempting to maintain good relations
with China out of fear of some military action. (In
this case these treaties might fall into the category
of "unequal treaties" as defined by Soviet international lawyers).[16] The other possibility is that
Mongolia may simply be trying to take advantage of
her position and gain the greatest possible benefit
from both the Soviet Union and China while at the
same time maintaining as much independence as possible. Since 1966 PRC-Mongolian treaty frequency has
declined sharply to an average of only one per year
for the last six years included in this study. This
is the same average as Sino-Soviet treaties in recent
years and certainly represents a bare minimum between
contiguous States. This decline in treaty frequency
has been accompanied by Chinese verbal attacks on
Mongolia beginning in 1967 when negotiations broke
down concerning the implementation of the Sino-Mongolian
cultural-cooperation agreement.[17] Typical of the
verbal attacks is the following excerpt from an article on the Council for Mutual Economic Aid appearing
in the Peking Review:

> Recent disclosures show that, because of
> ruthless plunder by the Soviet revisionists,
> Mongolia's livestock raising has been ser-
> iously undermined and Mongolian revision-
> ist authorities had to blatantly order the
> people to eat wild animals or go meatless....

for a country known for its animal hus-
bandry, people going meatless is strange
news indeed. (emphasis added) [18]

Chinese rhetoric obviously reflects the same de-
terioration in relations with Mongolia as shown in
the decline of PRC-Mongolian treaty frequency.

China's leading treaty partner in the South Asian
area is Ceylon (Sri Lanka) with a total of 60 treaties. This is not surprising since each country has
what the other wants. "Ceylon is a food deficit area
with an exportable surplus of rubber..." [19] Since 43
of the treaties with Ceylon involve trade and a large
share of these are specific rice-rubber contracts,
it is obvious that the Sino-Ceylonese relationship is
primarily economic. Trade with China represents a
larger share of Ceylon's total foreign trade than it
does in the case of any other South or Southeast
Asian country. [20] China has also continued to promote
good relations with Ceylon in the form of aid, having
signed 13 treaties involving aid to that country.

Indonesia, prior to the overthrow of the Communist
government, had been a steady and frequent treaty
partner of Communist China. However, since 1965,
which was the peak year with 9 treaties, Indonesia
has signed no agreements with the PRC.

The difference in PRC attitude brought about by
the change from the Sukarno to the Suharto regime

in Indonesia is well illustrated by two statements
appearing in the Peking Review, one during each administration. In 1965, following Indonesia's withdrawal from the United Nations over the seating of
Malaysia on the Security Council, the Peking Review
lauded Indonesia's action as an effort to "overcome
difficulties and crush imperialism." The editorial
further stated that the People's Republic of China
firmly supported Sukarno's stand.[21] Compare this
with the opening statement of a 1968 Peking Review
editorial:

> Behind the facade of exchanging "trade
> representative agencies," according to
> a report from Djakarta, the Suharto-
> Nasution fascist military regime of In-
> donesia, running dog of U.S. imperialism,
> had glaringly stepped up collusion with
> the Chiang Kai-shek bandit gang, the
> sworn enemy of the Chinese people, thus
> following its U.S. master in the plot
> to create "two Chinas."[22]

In spite of Indonesia's potential value to the
PRC as a resource supplying nation and trading partner, it is obvious that ideological differences and
not economic considerations have dictated the relationship.

Burma, Nepal and Pakistan are the other 3 significant Third World Asia treaty partners having 35
37, and 34 agreements respectively. Following a four
year hiatus, treaty relations between the PRC and

Pakistan resumed in 1963, following closely on the
heels of the Sino-Indian border war of October, 1962.
Pakistan is the sixth ranking treaty partner of the
PRC in the 1963 to 1972 period, gaining considerably
from its 17th ranking over the entire period from
1949 to 1972. It is apparent that Peking is comfor-
table in having friendly relations with Pakistan
based most assuredly on pragmatic concerns arising
out of the Sino-Indian tension. As further evidence
of the motivation for China's friendship with Pakistan,
Albert Feuerwerker cites the PRC's Security Council
veto on the admission of Bangladesh to the United
Nations in 1972. He notes that,

> It was China's perception of its immediate
> national interests against the Soviet Union
> and India, rather than revolutionary ideo-
> logy, which led to this support of its most
> unrevolutionary ally, Pakistan.[23]

After rather high treaty frequency between the
PRC and Burma through the mid-1960's there were no
treaties concluded between these neighboring countries
from 1966 until 1971. Strained relations caused by
alleged PRC supported communist insurrections in Burma and negative Burmese actions toward China, such as
the attack on the Chinese embassy in Rangoon in 1967,
account for the sudden absence of treaties during this
five year period.[24] Renewed Sino-Burmese relations
were marked by the signing of three treaties in 1971

on the topics of trade and aid and the signing of a single treaty in 1972 on cultural cooperation.

With the exception of 1969 and 1970, the years most affected by the Cultural Revolution, Nepal has maintained steady treaty relations with the PRC. Since the 1962 Sino-Indian Border clash, both the PRC and India have attempted to befriend the Nepalese, both governments granting technical assistance and aid to Nepal.[25] With the exception of some incidents in 1967 Sino-Nepalese relations have gone smoothly, as their treaty relations indicate.[26]

In the sub-Saharan African group, Guinea is the PRC's leading treaty partner. Diplomatic relations were established with Guinea in October, 1959. Earlier in 1958 and 1959, China had made some gifts of rice to Guinea. In September of 1960 President Sékou Touré visited Peking, where he signed a treaty of friend-ship, along with two other agreements for economic aid and trade. This was the first commitment for aid that Communist China had made to an African country.[27] The other two leading treaty partners in the African grouping are Mali with 25 treaties and Ghana with 17.[28] However, Tanzania, with 16 treaties all in the last ten-year period ranks very close to Mali in importance as a treaty partner. The first PRC-Tanzanian treaty was a cultural cooperation agreement, the first of

its kind to be signed by Tanzania.[29] Of great importance to both the PRC and Tanzania were six treaties
concluded in 1968 concerning the construction of the
Tanzanian-Zambian railway with Chinese aid and technical assistance. The project, completed in 1974, represented a significant accomplishment for the Chinese
in terms of prestige aid. It is interesting to note
that in 1974 Tanzania also completed a highway to
Zambia using U.S. aid.

Among the Arab countries there are no significantly large treaty partners for China. The UAR is
China's leading partner in this grouping with a total
of 23 treaties, or approximately 20% of the Arab
groups total treaties with the PRC. Another 12 treaties may be added to this total for the 1954-56 and
recent "Egypt" periods. Following the UAR are Syria and
Iraq with 17 and 15 treaties respectively. There are no
Arab States in the PRC's top twenty treaty partners either
for the entire time period or in the last ten year
period.

In the Western world Finland is by far the leading treaty partner with China, having a total of 30
agreements, all in the area of trade. Finland was
among the first Western States to conclude treaties
with the PRC having concluded their first in 1952.
(See Appendix Table 2) It is interesting to note that

until very recently Finland was the leading treaty
partner of the U.S.S.R., not just among Western nations, but in the entire world.[30]

Japan is a significant treaty partner also, but
the agreements with Japan have all been in the form of
semi-official documents. Though Japan did not officially recognize China, over 50 agreements have been
concluded between China and various unofficial commissions in Japan, many of which are composed of members
of the Japanese Diet.[31] On September 29, 1972 Japan
and the PRC agreed to resume diplomatic relations.

France is the next ranking partner with only 7
treaties. The United States has concluded only one
agreement with China, i.e., the controversial Agreed
Measures on Return of Civilians in 1955.[32]

Treaty Frequency by Topics

In looking at the overall topic distribution for
the entire 1,660 treaties, we find the following:
"Trade and Payments" is the largest general category
with a total of 679 treaties or approximately 41% of
the total treaties. The next leading topic is
"Health, Education, Culture, Welfare and Labor" with
490 treaties or 30% of the total. The leading sub-
topics in this category are Culture and Scientific
Projects. The other topic categories in order of

magnitude are: "Foreign Aid and Developmnnt Assistance" with 186 treaties; "Transportation and Communications" with 178 treaties; "Ad Hoc Dispositions of
Particular Matters" with 60 treaties; "Diplomatic, Administrative, and Judicial Cooperation" with 58 treaties; and "Military, War and Occupation" with 9
treaties.

Table 8 compares PRC and UNTS treaties by frequency of topic. For the world as a whole, aid is the
largest treaty topic, followed by trade, while for
Communist China, trade is the leading topic with 679
treaties. Health, education and welfare is the second
largest category (490) and aid is a distant third
(186). There are at least three factors contributing
to this difference between leading topics for the
PRC and leading topics globally. One is that the
single largest number of aid treaties (41%) of the
global total are contributed by the United States.
Secondly, the aid category in the UNTS includes aid
treaties by intergovernmental organizations which
are absent in China's treaties. China has been an
aid recipient as well as an aid donor but has never
received aid from an international organization.
Thirdly, until very recently China has not been in
a good position to give aid and the treaties in
which she received aid make up only a small part

of the total PRC aid and assistance category. It
should be noted, however, that this category is increasing rapidly over time with over 25% of all PRC
aid treaties having been signed since 1969. All of
these treaties are, of course, China-as-aid-donor
treaties.

Table 9, which indicates distribution by country
groupings gives yet another viewpoint of Chinese
treaties. For the Soviet-Core-Bloc countries as well
as for the PRC-Bloc countries the leading topic category is H.E.W. Totals for all Communist nations show
379 treaties in H.E.W. and only 315 treaties in Trade
which is the leading category in overall PRC treaties.

For the Arab, Asian and African groups combined,
Trade is overwhelmingly the largest topic, with 287
treaties of a total 600 treaties.

As far as the Western nations are concerned, the
preponderance of treaties is in the area of trade.
In actual numbers, trade accounts for 77 of the 103
treaties or 75% of the total signed with this country
group.

In Aid, the PRC-Bloc countries Albania, North
Korea and North Vietnam have the highest percentage
of aid treaties, nearly 36%. Next is the Asian group
with slightly over 25%. In actual numbers the PRC-
Bloc has 66 treaties, Asia 47 treaties and Africa 37

TABLE 8

DISTRIBUTION OF TREATIES BY TOPIC
PRC and UNTS

Topic #	Topic Description	PRC Treaties #	PRC Treaties %	UNTS Treaties #	UNTS Treaties* %
1.	Diplomacy-Administration	58	3%	1,219	14%
2.	Health, Education, Welfare Coop.	490	30%	1,039	12%
3.	Trade-Payments	679	41%	1,496	17%
4.	Aid and Assistance	186	11%	2,034	23%
5.	Transportation-Communication	178	11%	1,039	12%
6.	Military and Occupation	9	1%	1,017	12%
7.	International Organizations	0	0	484	6%
8.	Ad Hoc Matters	60	4%	313	4%
	Total	1,660		8,641	

* UNTS treaty information taken from Peter H. Rohn, Institutions
in Treaties: A Global Survey of Magnitudes and Trends from 1945
To 1965, See footnote 13, Chapter 1.

TABLE 9

TREATY FREQUENCY BY TOPIC
FOR VARIOUS STATE GROUPINGS

	General Topic Area							
	1	2	3	4	5	6	8	Totals
Communist Bloc								
Core-Bloc	7	210	156	8	35	0	2	418
PRC-Bloc	6	104	91	66	49	3	10	329
Yugosl-Cuba	3	19	34	2	11	0	0	69
USSR	6	46	34	16	18	1	20	141
Totals	22	379	315	92	113	4	32	957
Third World								
Asia	24	35	149	47	36	3	18	312
Arab	2	26	67	9	9	0	0	113
Africa	5	45	71	37	14	2	1	175
Totals	31	106	287	93	59	5	19	600
Western Nations	5	5	77	1	6	0	9	103
TOTALS	58	490	679	186	178	9	60	1,660

Topic 7 - International Organizations has been omitted as there are no PRC bilateral treaties in this category.

treaties of the total 186 Aid treaties.

The Soviet Union was the leader in this category until 1960, but there have been no Soviet Aid treaties since that time. Neither have there been any Aid treaties with any of the Core-Bloc countries except Romania, again indicating the effects of the Sino-Soviet dispute on the other countries within the bloc. The Sino-Soviet dispute has affected all topics in Chinese treaties with the Soviet Union.

Considering China's three leading treaty partners Albania, North Korea and North Vietnam individually, it can be seen that there has been a significant increase in all topics except Military and Ad Hoc Matters. This increase is probably also due to the fact that China has broadened her treaty horizons in all topics away from the Soviet Union in the period 1960-72.

In addition to the broad comparative overview of treaty frequencies by country groupings and topics presented above, it will be instructive to examine the trends of each country group separately. This should help account for some of the changes in treaty patterns through the years. The country groupings will be discussed in order of importance as determined by treaty volume.

The Soviet Union-Core Bloc

With the exception of 3 treaties concluded between the PRC and North Korea in 1949, the Soviet
Union and its satellite States, were the first countries to conclude treaties with the People's Republic
of China. In 1950, Czechoslovakia, East Germany, Poland and the Soviet Union all signed treaties with
the PRC (See Appendix Table 2). These 4 Communist
States accounted for 22 of the total 23 treaties
concluded by the PRC in its first full year of existence. The other treaty was concluded by North
Korea. The Soviet Union accounted for 19 of the
treaties in 1950, one each being concluded by the
other three Core Bloc countries. The major portion
of the Sino-Soviet agreements had to do with the
settlement and disposition of certain Soviet held
properties within the PRC. Most of the property and
territory had been acquired by the Soviet Union as a
result of the Japanese surrender in 1945. Other
treaties in this initial year of Sino-Soviet treaty
relations dealt with trade and aid to the PRC.

The Soviet Union alone has concluded a total of
141 treaties with the PRC. The other 6 States which
are included in this country group have concluded a
total of 418 treaties with the PRC from 1949 through

1972. The average number of treaties for this group
(excluding the Soviet Union) is 69.4. All countries
cluster rather closely around this average score.
Poland has concluded the largest number of treaties
with the PRC (78) and Bulgaria the fewest (57).
Fluctuations in treaty volume for this group of
States co-varies almost exactly with the PRC-Soviet
treaty frequency. Although it is no surprise, it is
but another indicator of how closely aligned these
States are with the Soviet Union. The one exception
to this common pattern has been Romania. Romania
ranks 6th among all PRC treaty partners for the entire period but for the last ten years it ranks 4th
among all partners. It is the only Core-Bloc country
(including the Soviet Union) to increase its ranking
in the past ten years compared to the rankings for
the overall period. For the past ten years the next
ranking Core-Bloc countries are East Germany and Poland in 10th and 11th places. The Soviet Union has
dropped to 14th in the rankings.

Since 1966 Romania has adopted an ever increasingly independent attitude vis-a-vis the Soviet
Union. On August 22, 1965, Romania adopted a new
constitution proclaiming itself to be a Socialist
State and no longer a People's Republic. During
this period Romania has been growing closer to the

PRC. While the Sino-Soviet rift has caused Soviet-PRC treaty frequency to decline sharply it has had a markedly different effect on Romanian-PRC treaty frequency. Since 1965, the beginning of Romanian-Soviet disenchantment, Romania has concluded 21 treaties with the PRC. The Soviet Union during the same period has concluded only 8 treaties with China. More importantly the trend for Romania shows an increase over time while the Soviet Union shows a decline.

Further, a look at the "treaty profile" for the Soviet Union shows Romania to be the eleventh ranking treaty partner of the U.S.S.R., but this relatively high rank was achieved as a result of a large number of treaties prior to 1961.[33] It is also significant that since the late 1950's the United States has also become a significant treaty partner with Romania, now ranking fifth among all Romanian treaty partners.[34]

Nearly one-third of the treaties concluded during this period between Romania and the PRC have been on the topic of aid, in the form of material goods and loans. It is evident that the PRC is quite willing to step into any breach created between the Soviet Union and its satellite States.

Romania provides a particularly good chance for

the PRC to gain political ground through the granting
of aid as it is one of the poorest of the Core-Bloc
countries. Its per capita GNP for 1970 was $930.[35]
Only Bulgaria is lower among these States with a per
capita GNP of $760. Correlations of per capita GNP
and treaty frequency within this group however yield
no significant relationship (r_s=.315) thus indicating
that within the Core-Bloc group treaty frequency
shifts can be attributed more to politics than eco-
nomics.

Probably as a result of the recent intensified
PRC interest, the Soviet Union has sought to improve
its economic relations with Romania in 1972.

PRC-Bloc

The country group having the second largest
volume of treaties with the PRC includes only 3 countries, North Korea, North Vietnam and Albania. This
group has the highest average number of treaties per
country. The Democratic Republic of Vietnam leads
this group with a total of 121 treaties for the entire time period. This is only 20 less than for
the Soviet Union. In overall treaty volume, North
Vietnam, North Korea and Albania rank 2,3 and 4 respectively and account for nearly 20% of the total
PRC treaty volume. For the period covering the

last 10 years, North Vietnam is the PRC's leading
treaty partner with 53 treaties followed by Albania
with 47 and North Korea with 46. North Korea is the
PRC's oldest treaty partner, being the only one to
sign treaties with the PRC in 1949.[36] The first
treaty with North Vietnam was concluded in 1952 and
the first with Albania in 1954.[37]

These three countries account for the largest
portion of treaties in 3 rather significant categories: Foreign Aid, Transportation and Communication,
and Military. The military treaties consist of military aid in 1971 to North Korea and recent military
aid to North Vietnam. PRC-Korean war settlement
treaties are not included as they are multilaterial
in nature. The PRC has signed 2 treaties on the
topic of military aid to North Vietnam. The first
treaty was signed on October 6, 1970 and the second
on January 22, 1972. It is interesting that these
military aid treaties, the first with Vietnam, should
come during the de-escalation of the Vietnam War and
during a period of growing PRC-United States detente.
This of course does not mean that the PRC has re-
frained from giving military assistance to North Vietnam during the entire period of the Vietnam War. Indeed, the following quote from an official Chinese
government statement appearing in the Peking Review

indicates that this is undoubtedly the case.

> China and Vietnam are neighbors as
> closely related as lips and teeth and
> are the most intimate fraternal so-
> cialist countries. China has consis-
> tently and unreservedly done its ut-
> most to support and aid Vietnam poli-
> tically, morally and materially and
> in other fields. The development by
> U.S. imperialism of its war of aggres-
> sion to a new and still graver stage
> has now further freed us from any
> bounds or restrictions in rendering
> such support and aid.[38] (emphasis added)

It is likely that the absence of formal public

treaties concerning military aid to Vietnam from the

PRC indicates a desire on the part of the PRC to re-

main, in so far as possible, formally uncommitted in

the Vietnam War until the full extent of U.S. inten-

tions in the area were clear. Once the "deescalation"

of the war had begun Peking could publicly commit

itself to military aid to Hanoi without fear of U.S.

action. There were certainly no advantages to be

gained by the PRC by another Korea-like confrontation

with the U.S. It should also be noted that the bulk

of the Vietnam War was fought during a period of inter-

nal political crisis for the PRC, culminating in the

Cultural Revolution. The Sino-Vietnamese military aid

treaties were concluded in the post Cultural Revolu-

tionary recovery period.

There are no known treaties with Albania on the

subject of military affairs. This is probably due

to the fact that Albania's geographic location makes
it relatively safe from any direct Soviet military
intervention. In addition, the granting of military
aid to Albania could be viewed as a hostile action
on the part of the PRC by the Soviet Union and Albania's close neighbors, Greece and Yugoslavia.
Since 1971 Albania has resumed diplomatic relations
with both of these countries and probably does not
wish to look as if it is building its military capa-
bilities significantly.[39]

In the category of Foreign Aid, these three
countries represent some rather striking statistics.
They account for 66 out of a total number of 186
treaties in the Aid category or 35.5%. However, the
total Aid category represents both those treaties
through which the PRC has received aid and those in
which it has granted aid. All treaties through
which the PRC received aid were concluded with the
Soviet Union, therefore subtracting their total of
16 treaties in the aid category we are left with a
total of 170 treaties in which the PRC has granted
aid to various countries. The PRC-Bloc countries
account for nearly 39% of this total.

In the extension of credits and grants by the
PRC to all countries, during the period from 1953 to
1965, North Vietnam, North Korea and Albania lead in

actual dollar values with $457 million, $330 million and $164 million respectively.[40] This is approximately 46% of the total credits and grants given to all countries for this period. This is a clear indicator of the value of treaty frequencies in various categories as an index of certain international behavior, especially since the treaties preceded the actual disbursement of aid, and therefore have predictive value on State behavior.

Asia

The Asian country grouping consists of a total of nine non-Communist Asian States and Mongolia. This group has an average treaty volume with the PRC of 31.2 per country, and accounts for approximately 19% of the PRC's total treaty volume. This country group leads in 2 topic categories: Diplomacy/Administration (topic 1) and Ad Hoc Matters (topic 8) and is second in 2 categories: Trade (topic 3) and Aid (topic 4).

It is not surprising that this group should have the most treaties with the PRC in topic category 8 since boundary agreements are included in this category and since 7 of the 10 countries share a common border with the PRC. The high volume in topic category 1 is probably also attributable to the high de-

gree of contiguity with the PRC, since as mentioned earlier, States have a normal proclivity to conclude more treaties in general with contiguous States.

The largest single category for this country group is Trade (149 treaties). This is second only to the Core-Bloc group with 156 treaties. Further, whereas the trend for the Core-Bloc group is downward, the Asian group has increased their treaties in this topic over time. As mentioned previously a large portion of the trade agreements are accounted for by rice-rubber contracts with Ceylon. In addition to Ceylon, Indonesia up to 1965 had been a leading trade partner with the PRC. Exactly half (13 out of 26) of Indonesia's treaties with the PRC were on the subject of trade. Indonesia, like Ceylon, was valuable to the PRC for the supply of rubber. Although Ceylon is the leading trade partner with the PRC in terms of treaty volume, Indonesia was the leader in this group in terms of dollar value of total trade through 1965.[41]

In 1964, for example, Ceylon had a total of 4 trade treaties with the PRC and her total volume of trade equalled $64 million.[42] On the other hand, Indonesia signed no trade treaties in 1964 but had a total trade volume of $106 million.[43] Further, they had signed only one trade treaty the previous year.

While this apparently indicates that treaty

volumes are not always an accurate indicator of
trade, another explanation suggests itself. That is,
the variable which may have to be considered is that
of the formality of the agreement. In the case of
Indonesia trade negotiations were concluded in the
form of "agreements" (<u>hsieh-ting</u>) whereas with Ceylon most trade negotiations are concluded in the
form of "contracts" (<u>ho-t'ung</u>). What is suggested
then is that the more formal arrangements tend to
include larger actual dollar volumes and more commodities whereas the less formal arrangements are for
specific commodities and therefore result in lower
per treaty dollar volume.[44]

India and Pakistan present another interesting
picture within this country group. From 1951 to 1959
India was a fairly significant treaty partner with
the PRC. This situation obtained in spite of the two
fundamental differences between India and the PRC
which clouded their relationship from the very beginning. Those differences were over the Sino-Indian
border and over the legal status of Tibet. These
almost inseparable and possibly unresolvable issues
dated back as early as the 1914 Simla Conference,
which attempted to wrest Tibet from Chinese suzerainty. The so-called McMahon Line, establishing part
of the Indo-Chinese border also resulted from this

conference. As explained in Chapter IV above, the PRC rejects the binding force of the Simla Conference on the basis that the Chinese representative only initialed but did not sign the document.[45]

In spite of these factors, rather lively trade existed between these two large Asian States during the 1950's. Of the total of 16 treaties signed with India during this period, 11 were on the topic of trade. Primary among these trade agreements were contracts for delivery of rice and other grain to India.[46]

The remainder of the treaties were on various subjects many of which concerned Tibet, including the famous Agreement on Trade and Intercourse with Tibet signed on April 29, 1954.[47] It should be recalled that this treaty was the first treaty to include the Five Principles of Peaceful Coexistence, that had been enunciated by Indian Prime Minister Nehru earlier that year. The mutual proclamation of the Five Principles marked the height of the Sino-Indian detente in 1954. It also marked the most productive year in Sino-Indian treaty relations. Fifty percent (8 of 16) of the entire Sino-Indian treaty volume was accounted for in that year. From 1955 through 1959 the PRC and India signed only one treaty per year.

Sino-Indian relations came to an abrupt halt

with the outbreak of border fighting in the summer
and autumn of 1959, which had come on the heels of
the Tibetan crisis in the spring of the same year.
Since 1959 the PRC has concluded no treaties with
India. The border war of 1962 apparently sealed the
fate of Sino-Indian relations for some time to come.

During the period of Sino-Indian detente, Pakistan being a member of the UN, SEATO and CENTO maintained close relations with the West, especially with
the United States. The United States had provided
Pakistan with considerable military and economic aid
during this period. The U.S. temporarily suspended
aid to both Pakistan and India during the 1966 Kashmir dispute and aid to Pakistan was again suspended
in 1971. As of 1973 the U.S. again agreed to "non-
lethal" military aid to Pakistan. Pakistan has been
content to accept aid from both sides of the political spectrum, however, accepting considerable aid
from the PRC since 1963. What began as a typical,
if somewhat low-level, trade relationship between
contiguous States, developed significantly differently
in the post Sino-Indian Border War period.

The first Sino-Pakistani treaty was signed in
1952 on the subject of trade. It was a semi-official
agreement signed at the non-governmental International
Economic Conference in Moscow, April 3 through 12,

1952. The agreement was not listed in the TYC but was reported in the People's Daily (jen-min jih-pao) on April 20, 1952. The first official trade agreement was signed in Karachi on March 14, 1953.[48]

Treaty relations continued at a low level from 1952 to 1963. No agreements at all were concluded during the period 1959 through 1962. All agreements signed between 1952 and 1963 were on the subject of trade.

In 1963 the picture changed drastically between the PRC and Pakistan. With the 1962 border war with India and a strengthening of Soviet-Indian relations, the PRC felt it necessary to establish a closer relationship with Pakistan. This was facilitated by the Pakistani attitude during the 1962 border dispute. Harold C. Hinton explains,

> It appeared to Pakistan that India was
> exploiting an exaggerated fear of a
> Chinese invasion of India as a means of
> extracting military aid from the West
> on a scale sufficient to alter the mili-
> tary balance in the Indian subcontinent
> drastically, to the disadvantage of In-
> dia's major opponent which remained Pak-
> istan rather than the CPR.[49]

Pakistan was assured by the West that India would not be allowed to use her new arms strength against Pakistan but this was little reassurance in Rawalpindi. Indo-Pakistani, as well as Western Pakistani, relations worsened and correspondingly Sino-

Pakistani relations strengthened. From 1963 on, after a 4 year gap, Sino-Pakistani treaty frequency has
been approximately 4 per year. There has been an
unusually high percentage of aid treaties in the recent agreements concluded with Pakistan. Since 1963,
22% of all treaties are on the subject of foreign
aid.

Since 28 of the 34 Sino-Pakistani treaties have
been signed in the past 10 years, Pakistan has experienced a significant rise in the rankings among
all PRC treaty partners. For the entire time period
Pakistan ranks 17th but for the period 1963 to 1972
Pakistan ranks 6th among the PRC's treaty partners.

As a group the Asian States have declined in
treaty frequency. In the overall rankings only 6
of the 10 Asian States are included in the top 20.
In the rankings for the last ten years only 5 Asian
States appear in the top 20. This difference is
mainly attributable to the complete break in treaty
relations between the PRC and 2 of the Asian States
(India and Indonesia). Those countries that have
remained in the top 20 rankings are Ceylon, Pakistan,
Nepal, Mongolia and Afghanistan. Of these 5 States,
3 have increased their ranking: Ceylon (11th to 5th),
Pakistan (17th to 6th) and Nepal (15th to 8th). In
the case of Ceylon the gain represents an increase

in economic intercourse between the two States. With
Pakistan and Nepal, considering the vital strategic
position and low economic status of both countries,
the increase in treaty frequencies can only be attributed to the achievement of political gains by the
PRC.

Africa

The countries of sub-Saharan Africa hold special
interest for China as a result of several interrela-
ted functions. The PRC sees Africa as an area
wherein the world revolutionary struggle can be maintained with Chinese aid. PRC aid in these revolutionary struggles lends credibility to the PRC claim
to be a revolutionary State. Africa is also an area
where the PRC has succeeded in gaining recognition
and support from a large number of States at rather
small cost to the Chinese. Finally, Africa serves
as an area where the PRC can work directly against
both United States "imperialism" and Soviet "revi-
sionism."[50]

As a result, the PRC has, since beginning
of the 1960's, made an intensive effort to cultivate
friendly relations with many of the African nations.
Africa's total treaty volume of 175 treaties with the
PRC does not give an accurate picture of the impor-

tance of the African States in PRC treaty relations.
The African group was the last group to enter into
treaty relations with the PRC (see Appendix Table 2).
The first treaty signed with a sub-Saharan African
nation was with Sudan in 1956. The agreement, which
took the form of an exchange of notes, established
trade relations between the two States. It was
signed in Khartoum on April 12, 1956, only four
months after Sudanese Independence.[51] This follows
the pattern of most African States in their treaty
relations with China. The PRC has been anxious to
conclude treaties with the newly independent African
States as soon after their independence as possible.[52]

Guinea, for example, who is the PRC's leading
treaty partner in Africa, signed its first agreement with the PRC one year after its independence
on October 2, 1958.[53] In addition to being the
PRC's leading treaty partner in Africa with a total
of 38 treaties, Guinea was the first African State
to receive a commitment for aid from the PRC.[54]

During the early 1960's Ghana was a very important treaty partner for the PRC. During the period
from August 1961 to August 1965, the PRC and Ghana
concluded 17 agreements. The topics of the agreements centered mostly around trade and technical
assistance. The final agreement signed in Accra on

August 5, 1965, was a protocol calling for the dis-
patch of PRC military experts to Ghana.[55] Since the
fall of Nkrumah in early 1966 there have been no treaties between Ghana and the PRC. In fact, the National Liberation Council expelled all Chinese Communist advisers, teachers and technicians and severed
diplomatic relations on November 5, 1966.

At the apex of Sino-Ghanaian relations in 1965,
the total trade volume between the two countries
reached $20.4 million. After the termination of di-
plomatic relations in 1966 trade declined to only half
a million dollars in 1967. No new agreements have
been signed since 1965 and diplomatic relations have
not been reestablished.

Another African State which followed a pattern
similar to that of Ghana in its relations with the
PRC is Mali. During the Socialist regime of President Modibo Keita the PRC and Mali entered into a
total of 25 agreements. Of these 25 agreements, 8
were on the subject of aid in various forms to Mali.
They included economic and technical aid as well as
loans. Through 1965 the PRC had granted a total of
$19.6 million in aid to Mali.[56] Since the end of
Keita's regime by coup on November 19, 1968 the PRC
has concluded only 1 treaty with Mali on the subject
of trade. Mali and the PRC continue to have diplo-

matic relations.

The State to which the PRC has been most atten-
tive in recent years is Tanzania. Treaty relations
were established with Tanzania 2 months after the
federation of the States of Tanganyika and Zanzibar
on April 26, 1964 with the signing of an agreement
on Economic and Technical Cooperation.[57] Prior to
that the PRC had concluded an agreement on the topic
of cultural cooperation with Tanganyika on December 13, 1962.[58]

Tanzania has a total of 16 treaties with the
PRC, half of which are on the subject of aid. A
large portion of these concern aid in the construction of the Tanzania-Zambian railway. Tanzania is
the largest recipient of aid from the PRC in Africa.
Through 1965 they had received a total of $45.5 mil-
lion in aid from the PRC. Tanzania is one of only 2
countries in Africa that receives more aid from the
PRC than from either the United States or the Soviet
Union. PRC-Tanzanian trade has also been high and has
increased rapidly from $.1 million in 1962 to $19.7
million in 1968.[59] This amounted to over 5% of Tanzania's total trade for 1968.

The one other large volume treaty partner for
the PRC in Africa is the People's Republic of the
Congo (Brazzaville). In overall treaty volume the

Congo has 15 treaties with the PRC and ranks 29th
among all treaty partners for all time. However, all
of the Congo's treaties have been concluded since 1964.
Considering the last ten years of this study only 18
nations have concluded more treaties with the PRC.
The Congo is the only other nation in Africa whose
aid from the PRC exceeds that of either the Soviet
Union or the United States. Moreover, it is the only
nation whose aid from the PRC ($25.2 million) exceeds
those of both the United States ($4 million) and the
Soviet Union ($9 million) combined.

Overall PRC treaty volume with African States
began to increase rapidly in the 1960-61 period,
finally reaching its peak in the 1964-65 period. During 1964-65 the African States became the PRC's leading treaty partners.

George T. Yu points out:

> Diplomatically, the major thrust of China's
> campaign took place between 1960 and 1965.
> At the height of this period (1964-1965),
> Chou En-lai and Ch'en Yi visited Africa
> and more than 70 percent of China's known
> aid commitments were directed toward Africa.
> By 1965, China's successful campaign had
> won for it recognition from seventeen Afri-
> can states.[60]

Certainly treaty volume during this period adequately bears this out.

Another indicator of Africa's importance to the
PRC in international relations is the fact that it is

the only country group that did not experience a decline
in frequency   during the height of the Cultural Revolution. In fact treaty frequency during 1968-69 increased by 14% over the previous 2-year period. In 1968-
69 the African States were again the leading country
group, nearly doubling the volume experienced by any
other country group (see table 4). On all levels of
interaction, cultural, economic, political and military, relations with the African States continued without major disruption even during the height of the Cultural Revolution.[61]

Africa, then, continues to be one of the most
important areas for PRC foreign relations. In 1972
the PRC concluded 14 treaties with African States,
more than with any other country group.

The Western States

Treaty frequency with the Western States has
greatly increased in the past several years, although
the PRC has seemingly taken care not to develop any
great volume of treaties with any one single Western
State.

Trade is the leading topic among the Western
States. Nearly 75% of all treaties concluded between
the PRC and the West are on the topic of trade. This
is not surprising when one looks at the dollar volume
of trade with these States. In the period 1961

through 1964, three States, Australia, Canada and New
Zealand, accounted for the total dollar volume of imports to China from the non-Communist countries.[62]
This was largely accounted for by the importation of
grain from these three countries. China continues
to export rice as a cash crop and imports wheat for
its own use.

Japan presents a very special case among those
nations grouped in the Western State category. Japan
has concluded over 50 semi-official agreements with
the PRC. These agreements, which are concluded between "private" agencies in both countries, include
many topics which are normally reserved for government to government relations. They also include
many arrangements that normally are handled by private agencies. From the total only 15 semi-official
agreements have been selected for inclusion in the
study. The criterion for inclusion was whether or not
the semi-official agreement fell under the category
of affairs normally (i.e. between countries having
normal diplomatic relations) handled by governmental
institution. Included are topics such as regulation
of fishing zones, repatriation of Japanese war cri-
minals and trade.

Given Japan's close relationship with the United
States, her dealings with the PRC had to be maintained

on this semi-official sort of basis, at least prior to formal U.S.-PRC relations. It is therefore difficult to assess Sino-Japanese relations in terms of treaty volume. In this case, for example, there is no significant correlation between dollar volume of trade and actual treaty volume. This unusual situation, however, can probably be explained for the most part by the exogenous variable of political pressures from the U.S. It is, of course, difficult to measure the effect of this variable in this situation. It is almost a certainty that when relations are normalized between Japan and the PRC, the treaty volumes will become a more accurate measure of relations between these States.

Cuba/Yugoslavia

Cuba and Yugoslavia have been dealt with separately in this study in light of their very special relationships with the two major Communist powers. Both countries at different times in their lives as independent States have maintained rather close relationships with both the Soviet Union and the PRC. Cuba has been the closer of these two countries to the PRC and will be dealt with first.

The first treaty between the PRC and Cuba was signed on December 31, 1959, the same year that Fidel

Castro became Premier. This agreement took the form
of a contract (ho-t'ung) and was signed by the China
National Foodstuffs Export Company and the Cuban
Trade Authority. The contract was for the outright
purchase of Cuban sugar.[63] The first official agreements between the two countries were a trade and payments agreement and an agreement for scientific and
technical cooperation both signed in Havana on July
23, 1960.[64]

In view of a rice shortage in Cuba and a sugar
shortage in China, trade relations between the two
countries prospered. PRC trade volume with Cuba increased from $42 million in 1960 to $180 million in
1964.[65] Treaty volume for these years followed an
almost identical pattern with dollar volume of trade.

By 1965 however, Sino-Cuban relations had begun
to deteriorate primarily as a result of two factors.
First, this was a period of intensification of the
Sino-Soviet dispute and since Cuba had received a
great deal of aid from both parties it wished to avoid
taking sides in the dispute in so far as possible.
Second, the PRC as a result of a rather large sugar
crop in 1965 did not need to import a large volume
of Cuban sugar. In addition, the PRC refused to send
as much rice to Cuba as had been planned. As a result
of growing antagonisms between the two countries,

Fidel Castro, in a speech on January 2, 1966, denounced the PRC for "blackmail and extortion" for
cutting its rice shipments.[66]

Treaty volume declined sharply as a result of
the "rice-sugar" dispute and from 1967 to 1969 no
treaties were concluded between the two countries.
Only one treaty was signed in each year of 1969 and
1970, both on the subject of trade.[67] In 1971, however, relations appear to have improved again as
three agreements were signed, all in the area of trade.

Yugoslavia presents a rather different picture
than Cuba in its relations with the PRC. In overall
treaty volume with the PRC, Yugoslavia ranks 18th
among all partners with a total of 29 treaties. However, in the past ten years Yugoslavia has concluded
only 7 treaties with the PRC. The first 2 agreements
between Yugoslavia and the PRC were concluded on
February 14, 1956 on the topics of postal services
and telecommunications.[68] During 1956 and 1957 Yugoslavia and the PRC concluded a total of 16 treaties.
Since 1958 there has been an average of one treaty
per year concluded between these two States.

Several explanations suggest themselves for this
rather peculiar behavior in treaty relations. It will
be recalled that beginning in the mid-1950's pressures
between Yugoslavia and the Soviet Union began to grow.

It was in 1956 that Soviet troops invaded neighboring Hungary, no doubt causing a great deal of unrest
in Belgrade. It is suggested here that as in the current situation with Romania, the PRC saw an opportunity to strengthen its position among the non-Soviet
Communist States. At the same time Yugoslavia probably had a strongly felt need for support from the
other major Communist power. However, since that
time, while continuing reasonably friendly relations
with both the Soviet Union and the PRC, Yugoslavia
has continued to grow closer to the West, a move
which it began as early as 1948.[69] In 1970, Yugoslavia signed a trade agreement with the European
Common Market.

Several patterns emerge in the PRC treaty relations examined quantitatively in this chapter. First,
PRC treaty relationships seem to be dictated by a
peculiar mix of ideologically based motives and economic and political pragmatism. The effect on Soviet-
Core Bloc States by the Sino-Soviet dispute, Pakistani-
PRC treaty increases after the Sino-Indian war and
prestige aid treaties with the African States are but
a few examples. Second, it is clear from treaty patterns that the PRC has definitely established its
own communist bloc of States. Third, it is also
apparent that China is willing and able, to fill any

power vacuum left by the Soviet Union.

The PRC's treaty patterns, taken alone, show value as both retrospective indicators, as in the case of the Great Leap Forward and its effect on Sino-Soviet treaty frequency and as predictive indicators as in the case of PRC trade and aid treaties with various States and State groups. In the next chapter, treaty data will be combined with other quantitative behavioral indicators to enhance their value as both retrospective and predictive indices.

204

FOOTNOTES

1. See supra Ch. IV, pp. 110-112 for a discussion of PRC theory regarding those entities eligible
to conclude treaties.

2. For a detailed discussion of the Great Leap
Forward see for example, Franz Schurmann, Ideology and
Organization in Communist China, Berkeley, University
of California Press, 1969.

3. Morton Halperin, "Is China Turning In?," Harvard University, Center for International Affairs, No.
12, (December, 1965).

4. Daniel Tretiak, "Is China Preparing to 'Turn
Out'?: Changes in Chinese Levels of Attention to the
International Environment," Asian Survey, Vol. XI,
No. 3,(March, 1971), pp. 219-237.

5. Ibid., The average figure of 50.29% is taken
from Tretiak's breakdown of foreign news coverage by
the Peking Review into eight six-month time frames
from January 1966 through December, 1969. Tretiak's
percentages are as follows: January-June, 1966,63.03%:
July-December, 1966, 43.55%; January-June, 1967, 41.48%;
July-December, 1967, 53.55%; January-June, 1968,50.15%;
July-December, 1968, 48.40%; January-June, 1969,51.88%;
July-December, 1969, 50.28%.

6. The country groupings are as follows: Africa-
Burundi, Camaroon, Central Africa, Congo (Brazzaville),
Equatorial Guinea, Ethiopia, Ghana, Guinea, Kenya,
Malagasy, Mali, Mauritania, Mauritius, Rwanda, Sierra
Leone, Somalia, Sudan, Tanganyika-Tanzania, Togo, U-
ganda, Zambia; Arab-Algeria, Egypt(non-UAR), Iraq, Leba-
non, Morocco, Southern Yemen, Syria, Tunisia, UAR,
Yemen (Sana); PRC-Bloc-Albania, North Korea, North
Vietnam; Soviet Core-Bulgaria, Czechoslovakia, East
Germany, Hungary, Poland, Romania, USSR; West-Austria,
Belgium, Brazil, Canada, Chile, Denmark, Finland,
France, West Germany, Guyana, Hong Kong, Italy, Japan,
Malta, Mexico, Netherlands, Norway, Peru, Portugal,
Sweden, Switzerland, U.K., Uruguay, USA; Asia-Afghan-
istan, Burma, Cambodia, Ceylon, India, Indonesia, Laos,
Mongolia, Nepal, Pakistan, (Tibet). The inclusion of
Mongolia in the Asian group is not altogether satis-
factory, however, it was felt that Mongolia was more
"Asian" than "Communist" and Soviet or Chinese Bloc.
It is simply typical of the problems encountered when
trying to categorize all of the world's States.

7. Daniel Tretiak, "Pekings Policy Toward Sin-Kiang: Trouble on the New Frontier," Current Scene, Hong Kong, Vol. 24, No. 11, (November 15, 1963).

8. Statistics derived from Peter H. Rohn, Treaty Profiles, Santa Barbara, Calif., American Bibliographical Center, Clio Press, 1975.

9. For a thorough discussion of dual approach to the international community see Albert Feuerwerker, "Relating to the International Community," in Michel Oksenberg, ed., China's Developmental Experience, New York, Praeger, 1973, pp. 42-54.

10. Listed in Douglas M. Johnston and Hungdah Chiu, Agreements of the People's Republic of China, 1949-1967: A Calendar, Cambridge, Harvard Univ. Press, 1968, p. 29; The treaty is reported in Far Eastern Economic Review, Hong Kong, (January 19, 1961) p. 85.

11. "Courageous and Resolute Revolutionary Action," JMJP (Sept. 20, 1968) p. 1; English translation appears in Peking Review (Sept. 27, 1968); quoted in Jerome A. Cohen and Hungdah Chiu, People's China and International Law: A Documentary Study, Princeton, New Jersey, Princeton Univ. Press, 1974, p. 1282.

12. "The Leaders of the CPSU Are the Greatest Splitters of Our Times," JMJP, (Feb. 4, 1964) pp. 1-4; English translation appears in Peking Review, (Feb. 7, 1964); and in Cohen and Chiu, op. cit., pp. 140-143.

13. Robert C. North, The Foreign Relations of China, Belmont, California, Dickenson, 1969, pp. 130-132.

14. Harold C. Hinton, Communist China in World Politics, Boston, Houghton Mifflin, 1966, p. 330.

15. The New York Times, May 22, 1964.

16. Jan F. Triska and Robert M. Slusser, The Theory, Law and Policy of Soviet Treaties, Stanford, Stanford University Press, 1962, p. 23.

17. See Cohen and Chiu, op. cit., pp. 1161-1162. The Chinese embassy protest of Mongolia's actions as reported in "Embassy Protests New Mongolian Provocation," NCNA,- English, Peking, (Sept. 6, 1967)

18. "'Council for Mutual Economic Aid'-Soviet Revisionist Tool for Pushing Neocolonialism," Peking Review, (Feb. 14, 1969).

19. Hinton, op. cit., p. 462.

20. A. Doak Barnett, Communist China and Asia, New York, Vintage, 1960, p. 316.

21. "Indonesia Quits UN--A Just, Correct and Revolutionary Action," Chinese Government Statement, January 10, 1965, Peking Review, (Jan. 15, 1965).

22. "Indonesian Fascist Militarist Regime Steps up Collusion with Chiang Kai-shek Gang," Peking Review, (July 5, 1968); for a thorough treatment of the Sino-Indonesian rift and the relationship between the PRC, Indonesian government and the Indonesian Communist Party see Sheldon W. Simon, The Broken Triangle; Peking, Djakarta, and the PKI, Baltimore, Johns Hopkins Press, 1969.

23. Albert Feuerwerker, "Relating to the International Community," in Michel Oksenberg, ed., China's Developmental Experience, New York, Praeger, 1973, p.47.

24. See for example, Cohen and Chiu, op. cit., p. 1024; and "Chinese Embassy Protests against Burmese Governments Sabotage of Economic-Technical Cooperation Agreement," NCNA-English, Peking (July 6, 1967) in SCMP, no. 3977: 27-28 (July 11, 1967), appears also in Cohen and Chiu, op. cit., pp. 1106-1107.

25. See Joseph S. Roucek, "Nepal on a Tight Rope," Eastern World, Vol. 21, no. 5/6 (May/June 1967) pp. 10-11.

26. "Protest against Nepalese Government Connivance at Anti-China Outrage," Peking Review (July 14, 1967); also see Cohen and Chiu, op. cit., pp. 885-888.

27. Richard Lowenthal and Zbigniew Brzezinski, eds.,Africa and the Communist World, Stanford, Stanford University Press, 1963, pp. 165-167, 183-184.

28. Diplomatic Relations between Ghana and China were suspended on November 5, 1966.

29. TYC 11:123

30. Triska and Slusser, op. cit.

31. See Johnston and Chiu, Agreements of the People's Republic of China 1949-1965: A Calendar, Cambridge, Harvard University Press, 1968, passim for the various semi-official commissions. For a discussion of the nature of these agreements, see Adams, supra, Ch. I, note 13, pp. 250-251.

32. Subcommittee for National Security and International Operations, Problems of Negotiation with Communist China, Washington D.C., U.S. Government Printing Office, February, 1969.

33. Peter Rohn, op. cit.

34. Ibid.

35. UN Statistical Yearbook

36. TYC 1:150; TYC 1:155; TYC 1:160.

37. TYC 2:136; TYC 3:172.

38. "Chinese Government Statement: China's Aid to Vietnam in Fighting U.S. Agression Further Ceases to be Subject to Any Bounds or Restrictions," July 3, 1966, Peking Review, (July 8, 1966).

39. For a discussion of the PRC-Albanian alliance from two viewpoints see, Anton Logoreci, "Albania and China: The Incongruous Alliance," Current History, Vol. 52 no. 308 (April 1967) pp. 227-231; and "A New Peak in the Militant Friendship of the Chinese and Albanian Peoples," China Reconstructs, Peking, Vol. 18, No. 1 (Jan. 1969) pp. 16-17.

40. An Economic Profile of Mainland China, 2 Vols., Prepared for the Joint Economic Committee Congress of the United States, Washington, D. C., U.S. Government Printing Office, 1967, p. 589.

41. Ibid., p. 616.

42. Ibid.

43. Ibid.

44. It is realized that the orthodox view in international law is that titles of international instruments have no particular legal significance, what is

suggested is that there may be other than legal significance attached to the nomenclature of treaties.
For a quantitative study using a global treaty data
base supporting this assertion see Juris A. Lejnieks,
"The Nomenclature of Treaties: A Quantitative Analysis," The Texas International Law Forum, Vol. II,
No. 2, (Summer, 1966) pp. 175-188.

45. For the PRC position on the Sino-Indian Bor-
der see, The Sino-Indian Boundary Question, Peking,
Foreign Languages Press, 1962. See esp. Premier Chou
En-lai's, "Letter to the Leaders of Asian and African
Countries on the Sino-Indian Boundary Question" at
p. 15.

46. See for example, SCMP 99:2

47. TYC 3:1; The English Text of the Agreement
appears in UNTS 299:70. India registered the Agreement with the UN Secretariat on April 28, 1958.

48. TYC 2:9

49. Hinton, op. cit., p. 455.

50. George T. Yu, "China's Competitive Diplomacy in Africa," in Jerome A. Cohen, ed., The Dynamics
of China's Foreign Relations, Harvard Asian Monograph,
No.39, Cambridge, Harvard University Press, 1970,p.69.

51. TYC 5:59

52. Yu, op. cit., p. 70.

53. TYC 8:127

54. See supra, note 27

55. Reported in Ghana, Ministry of Information,
Nkrumah's Subversion in Africa, 1966, p. 56.

56. Yu, op. cit., p. 77.

57. Reported in JMJP, June 18, 1969.

58. TYC 11:123

59. Yu, op. cit., p. 77.

60. Ibid.

61. Ibid.

62. Economic Profile, op. cit., p. 648.

63. JMJP, January 12, 1960.

64. TYC 10:238; TYC 10:402.

65. Economic Profile, op. cit., p. 648.

66. Lee, op. cit., p. 86.

67. SCMP 4363 :19; SCMP 70-28 (4695)33.

68. TYC 5:174; TYC 5:182.

69. For a discussion of the peculiar role of Yugoslavia in treaty relations with both the Communist and Western countries see Peter H. Rohn, "A Computer Search in Soviet Treaties," The International Lawyer, Vol. 2, no. 4, (July 1968) pp. 661-680.

CHAPTER VI

TREATIES AND COMPARATIVE DATA

It has been asserted both implicitly and explicitly in the preceding chapters that treaties are one
of the important indicators by which we may judge and
even perhaps predict the behavior of a State in the
international system. It has been shown in certain
specific cases that treaties do indeed give us a rather accurate index of behavior. But, as Douglas M.
Johnston so correctly points out in his coveat concerning the use of PRC treaties as a predictor of
behavior,

> Legal inquiry into the predictability
> of Communist Chinese behavior before and
> after the fact of official commitment
> should proceed by way of functional analy-
> sis, focusing on the differentiation and
> overlapping uses to which the PRC's agree-
> ments have been put. [1]

It is suggested here that the type of functional
analysis that Professor Johnston suggests as well as
the reliability of treaties as behavioral indicators
generally can be enhanced to a great extent by using
quantitative treaty data in combination with, and
comparison to, other quantitative behavioral indicators. This chapter then will compare other indicators of State behavior, such as trade statistics,
foreign aid and other economic data, with treaty data

211

for the People's Republic of China in order to show
further that the generalization of treaties as indices of behavior holds true for PRC treaties as well.

In addition, the latter part of the chapter will
examine the trends and patterns of PRC treaties in
combination with certain events data both internal
and external to the PRC in order to attempt to explain the sometimes high degree of fluctuation in
the frequency of PRC treaties throughout the 1949 to
1972 period.

Foreign Aid

PRC treaties in the aid and assistance category involve China as both an aid recipient and an
aid donor country. Less than 10% of the PRC treaties
in this category are China-as-recipient treaties and
all but one of these treaties are with the Soviet
Union.

In its initial years, the PRC was the recipient
of large amounts of aid from the Soviet Union. Indeed the very heart of China's plan for rapid industrial expansion was early Soviet aid. The type of
aid given ranged from economic grants and loans to
the delivery of complete industrial plants to the
PRC. Under the original Soviet plan for aid, the
PRC was to receive, in connection with her forthcom-

ing three 5-year plans, a package of 130 industrial
plants having a total value of approximately $1.35
billion by 1959. By 1967, 291 major industrial
plants, valued at $3.3 billion, were to have been
transferred to the PRC, all in basic areas of industrial production.[2] Although some of the aid was in
the form of gifts, most was paid for by the PRC in
the transfer of food products and basic raw materials
to the Soviet Union. The Soviet Union also supplied
technical assistance in the form of advisers, technicians and technical information. It also made
available to the Chinese teaching facilities in the
U.S.S.R. which trained approximately 8,000 technicians and researchers and 7,000 academic students.[3]
The Soviets, in addition, extended small amounts of
financial aid, (approximately $1.4 billion in loans)
most of which was to be used for military purchases.[4]

The Sino-Soviet rift, which was intensified by
the launching of the Great Leap Forward and the demand for Soviet nuclear technology, brought an end
to Soviet aid to the PRC. The last Sino-Soviet aid
treaty was concluded on February 7, 1959.[5] By mid-
1960 the Soviet Union decided to withdraw all support from China, leaving many of the projects, agreed
upon prior to 1959, as yet not completed. Some were
still only in the planning stages. The total result

was the withdrawal of nearly 1,400 Soviet experts and
the negation by the Soviets of 257 projects of scientific and technical cooperation.[6]

In addition to the Soviet Union, the PRC also
received aid from East Germany in the supply of complete plants. The last aid agreement in which the
PRC was the recipient country was signed with East
Germany in March 9, 1959.[7]

The total aid category with the Core-Bloc countries, other than the Soviet Union, consists of only
8 agreements. With the exception of the 1959 agreement with East Germany, these all reflect aid from
the PRC to the other Core-Bloc countries. Romania
is the largest recipient of aid from the PRC in terms
of dollar volume and the most frequent treaty partner
in this area, having 6 of the total 8 treaties in the
Core-Bloc aid category. The aid has taken various
forms including technical assistance and the granting
of interest-free loans. All 6 of the aid treaties
with Romania have been concluded since 1970.

The PRC became an aid donor country as early as
1953, during the time when she was still an aid
recipient country, and still in the midst of her own
reconstruction. The first treaty in which the PRC
gave aid was an agreement involving the extension of
noncommercial credit to Mongolia on February 24, 1953.[8]

During the period 1953 to 1957, the PRC also expanded
its aid program to a number of non-Communist developing States. It became the pattern for the PRC to
attempt to promote trade and political gain through
the prior granting of aid to various countries. According to one source, PRC aid to non-Communist developing States in 1956 and 1957 may have reached as
high as $72 million.[9] A more conservative estimate
places it around $30 million per year in the 1956-
1959 period.[10] The chief recipients of this early
aid were Egypt, Indonesia, Ceylon, Nepal and Cambodia.

The total aid given by the PRC during the 1953-
57 period was approximately $500 million. Though this
amount may seem low in contrast to amounts of aid normally given by Western aid donor countries, it must
be remembered that the PRC was in the midst of its own
economic reconstruction and the aid given represented
a reasonably large share of its domestic product.[11]

Although early Chinese aid was focused essentially on contiguous Asian States, since 1960 the PRC
has expanded its aid program considerably to Africa
and the Middle East. Since 1960 the average annual
aid extensions to non-Communist countries have risen
to approximately $125 million. By 1965 the number
of non-Communist aid recipients had expanded to 21.[12]

The dollar volume of PRC aid to non-Communist

States by 1965 had reached $850 million, slightly
over 50% going to Asian States, over 30% to Africa
and the remainder to the Arab group. As Milton Kovner notes, the PRC's aid program to the non-Communist
world stands as "striking testimony to its readiness
to sacrifice ideological consistency to political advantage."[13] Aid treaty volume for these non-Communist State groups also follows a very similar distribution pattern. Asia has concluded 50.5 % of the aid
treaties among this group combination, Africa has concluded 39.7% and the Arab States the remainder. What
disparity does exist between dollar volume aid statistics and treaty volumes, i.e. with the African
and Arab States, is probably accounted for by the
much larger number, yet smaller States, in the African group, thereby requiring higher treaty frequencies for the distribution of similar dollar amounts.

The PRC's foreign aid program has somewhat of a
paradoxical nature in view of China's own rather peri-
lous internal economic situation. With a per capita
GNP of only $160 for 1970 the PRC is in the position
of granting economic aid to many countries in better
financial situations than her own. In fact, nearly
half of the countries receiving aid from China have
a per capita GNP equal to or above that of the PRC.
Of the PRC's 3 closest allies (the PRC-Bloc) and

largest recipients of aid from the PRC, only North
Vietnam has a lower per capita GNP than the PRC. Albania and North Korea are far above with $330 and
$600 per capita GNP.

The most striking difference is represented by
Romania which has concluded the largest number of aid
treaties with the PRC since 1970 (6), and has a per
capita GNP of $930, nearly 6 times that of the PRC.
Measured by standards of per capita GNP with the exception of India, the PRC is undoubtedly by far the
poorest among the world's large aid donor nations,
(see table 10 on page 218). Comparative figures for
1970 show that the PRC gave approximately the same
percent of aid to total GNP as did the United States.
(see table 11 on page 219). Paraphrasing Kovner, the
PRC seems to be sacrificing "economic consistency"
for ideological and political advantage.

The question arises; why does the PRC follow such
a seemingly irrational practice in light of its own
internal financial predicament? Several possibilities
present themselves for a synthesis in answer to the
question.

First, the PRC has borrowed much of its economic
planning from the Soviet Union, most especially in
the sense of ordering their economic priorities.
Therefore when the goals of industrial expansion and

TABLE 10

RANKING OF AID DONOR STATES BY PER CAPITA GNP - 1970[*]

and by TOTAL AID GIVEN

Rank by Per Cap. GNP	Country	Per Cap. GNP in U. S. Dollars	Rank by Total Aid Given
1	U.S.A.	4,760	1
2	Sweden	4,040	13
3	Canada	3,700	8
4	Switzerland	3,320	15
5	Denmark	3,190	16
6	France	3,100	3
7	West Germany	2,930	5
8	Norway	2,860	19
9	Australia	2,820	10
10	Belgium	2,720	11
11	East Germany	2,490	14
12	Netherlands	2,430	9
13	United Kingdom	2,270	4
14	Czechoslovakia	2,230	22
15	Austria	2,010	21
16	Japan	1,920	2
17	U.S.S.R.	1,790	12
18	Italy	1,760	6
19	Hungary	1,600	18
20	Poland	1,400	23
21	Romania	970	24
22	Bulgaria	760	17
23	Portugal	660	20
24	PRC	160	7

* Data taken from United Nations Statistical Yearbook - 1972

TABLE 11

RANKING OF AID DONOR STATES BY % of AID PER TOTAL GNP

1970*

Rank	Country	TOTAL AID GIVEN (Millions of U.S.$	% of AID PER TOTAL GNP
1	Netherlands	449	1.42
2	Bulgaria	82	1.26
3	Portugal	69	1.20
4	Australia	425	1.18
5	Belgium	285	1.08
6	France	1,646	1.06
7	United Kingdom	1,175	.93
8	Japan	1,762	.88
9	Italy	690	.73
10	Canada	557	.70
11	West Germany	1,145	.66
12	Norway	72	.64
13	Sweden	183	.57
14	U.S.A.	5,442	.56
15	PRC	685	.55
16	Switzerland	113	.54+
17	Denmark	85	.54-
18	Hungary	79	.48
19	Austria	67	.45
20	East Germany	125	.31
21	Czechoslovakia	55	.17
22	Poland	25	.054
23	Romania	10	.053
24**	U.S.S.R.	197	.46

* Data taken from United Nations Statistical Yearbook - 1972

** Aid given by the Soviet Union in 1970 was approximately one-third of their yearly average aid output

great power status are established, there is every
willingness among the leaders to divert capital from
the sector of the economy producing consumer goods
and services into those sectors which more directly
serve to produce the desired goals.

Aid serves as one method which the Chinese leadership views as important in serving these ends.
The PRC has consistently directed the use of aid to
develop trade. This is evident by comparing the number of aid treaties with the number of trade treaties
in each of the countries to which recent PRC aid has
been granted. Considering the countries in the PRC-
Bloc, Asian, African and Arab groups we find an extremely high Spearman rank order correlation between
volume of aid treaties and volume of trade treaties,
$(r_s = .796)$, thus indicating a reasonably high degree
of success, at least in terms of trade treaty volume.

Another factor that has caused the PRC to extend
itself in the granting of aid has to do with its own
self image. In spite of continued Chinese protesta-
tions to the contrary the overwhelming evidence of
Chinese actions would seem to indicate that the PRC
envisions itself as one of the great powers of the
world and therefore in direct competition with both
the Soviet Union and the United States for world leadership. [14] The Sino-Soviet rift has only served to

exacerbate this competition.

There has been a great deal of competition with the Soviet Union in the area of foreign aid, most especially in the newly independent developing nations. Many Chinese and Soviet loans have followed on the heels of one another. As noted by Floyd, "The extension of a $35 million loan by Russia to the new state of Guinea in Africa was followed by one of $25 million from the Chinese."[15] Of course the PRC is unable to compete with the Soviets in terms of total dollar amounts of aid, but they have made exceptionally good use of what they are able to give by creating more liberal repayment schedules for their loans and by quite often granting interest free loans. The PRC does not fail to point up the differences between their methods and those of the Soviets.[16]

Chinese foreign aid figures show a very similar trend to their treaty patterns. Holsti and Sullivan show that there has been a steady decline in intra-bloc aid since 1960 while non-bloc aid for the same period has increased.[17] As noted previously, treaty frequency with the Soviet Union and the Core-Bloc countries has steadily declined since the 1958-59 period.

Nearly all Chinese aid within the Communist system (Soviet-Core Bloc and PRC-Bloc countries), since

the Sino-Soviet rift, has been granted to countries which support the Chinese position against that of the Soviet Union. The treaty patterns within the Communist system have followed precisely this same pattern. Since 1960 the Soviet Union has concluded only 38 treaties with the PRC. On the other hand the PRC has concluded 66 treaties with North Vietnam, 62 treaties with Albania and 59 treaties with North Korea during the same period.

Outside the Communist system, foreign aid seems to be given generally to countries which the Chinese feel will support their position against India and/or the United States. A very good illustration of this can be seen with Pakistan. Prior to the Sino-Indian border clash in 1962, the PRC had supplied no aid to Pakistan and had signed no treaties with her since 1958. However, treaty relations resumed in 1963, and in 1964, the PRC extended $60 million in economic aid to Pakistan. There can be no doubt that Sino-Indian and Pakistani-Indian animosities were the prime motivating factor behind this politically and ideologically strange friendship.

In the competition with the United States as well as the Soviet Union, the PRC is lagging rather far behind. The aid category for the PRC comprises only 11% of its total 1660 treaties. If we exclude those

treaties in which she received aid, the PRC aid donor
treaties then comprise only 9.8% of its total treaty
volume. This compares rather unfavorably with the
United States whose aid treaties comprise approximately
one-third of the entire American treaty universe.

This disparity in competition is, of course, only
exaggerated by comparing actual dollar volume of aid
in comparison to aid treaties. The African group in
which the United States, the Soviet Union and the PRC
all compete will serve as an example.

Through 1965 the PRC had concluded 21 aid treaties
with the African group (approximately 16% of the PRC's
total aid category at the time). Total aid granted by
the PRC to the African group in the same time period
totaled $350.4 million. The United States, on the
other hand, had concluded 67 aid treaties with the
African group representing a total dollar volume of
nearly $3 billion. The Soviet Union's aid contribu-
tion to Africa during this same period was slightly
over $1.5 billion. Thus while the United States con-
cluded only about three times as many aid treaties
with Africa as did the PRC, they granted nearly ten
times the dollar amount in aid.[18]

Several conclusions can be drawn about PRC foreign aid in relation to its treaty volume. First, internally, aid treaties represent a meaningful index of

Chinese intent and purpose, if not of their successes.
They are a reasonably accurate gauge as to the PRC's
aid dollar flow to other countries, or at least of
commitment of dollar amounts, (i.e. portions of aid
extended by the PRC have not been utilized by recipient States).

Second, they are also a reasonable predictor of
Chinese intent to create trade since most aid projects are tied to the purchase of Chinese goods.[19]
At times, however, the intended trade does not materi-
alize to the degree that may be intended. Tanzania,
for example, is one of the two African nations in
which PRC aid exceeds either U.S. or Soviet aid yet
in 1968 trade between the PRC and Tanzania accounted
for only slightly more than 4% of Tanzania's total
trade with all partners.[20] That is not altogether
surprising, however, since the aid-trade sequence is
likely to take a few years to develop. In addition,
according to George T. Yu, Tanzanian trade patterns
still tend to be governed by traditional relationships.[21]

Third, PRC aid treaties give a somewhat exaggerated view of the PRC as a donor nation in terms of
dollar amounts in comparison to other aid donor States.
Moreover, its total dollar amount of aid, while more
accurate for comparative purposes, nonetheless gives

a somewhat distorted picture of the PRC's actual ability , in terms of per capita GNP, to be a large donor
nation. What PRC aid treaties do tend to reflect accurately, in comparison to other States, is the percent of total GNP commited for aid.

Finally from these somewhat disparate conclusions about the PRC's aid treaties and aid dollars we
can synthesize one very positive conclusion. That
is, that PRC aid treaties reflect accurately the
PRC's intentions to play a major role in international affairs both in the group of countries known
as the third world and in competition with the Soviet
Union for political advantage in the communist world.

Trade Statistics

Another indicator of China's foreign relations
are her trade statistics. Like foreign aid, China
has concentrated her efforts in the area of trade in
order to strengthen her economy. She has also used
trade to pursue the political objectives of achieving
great power status and a leadership position in Asia
and the third world in general.

In general trade statistics, in terms of dollar
volumes, follow a pattern reasonably close to that of
trade treaties. For the period from 1950 through 1965
the PRC concluded a total of 491 trade treaties. The

total dollar volume of trade during this same period
was nearly $45 billion. The lowest dollar volume year
for trade was 1950 with only $1.21 billion. It was
also the lowest year for trade treaties, i.e. only
six. By dividing this 16 year period into 2-year
time periods we get a fairly high Spearman rank-order
correlation between number of trade treaties concluded
in each period and actual trade volume (r_s = .548).
Since trade treaties reflect an <u>intent</u> to trade, rather than actual trade, it might be expected that treaties should be predictive of, rather than reflective of,
trade volume. In other words the best correlation
ought to be obtained between present treaty frequency
and future trade volume. I therefore projected the
treaty frequency of each two-year period onto the
following two-year period for trade volume for the
same total time frame considered above. Thus the ranking of the 1950-51 two-year treaty period was correlated with the 1952-53 two-year trade volume period and
the 1952-53 treaty period with the 1954-55 trade period, etc. The result was a considerably improved
correlation coefficient (r_s = .714). The significantly
higher correlation obtained from this method of projection indicates that PRC trade treaty frequency is
an excellent predictive indicator of future PRC
trade volume.

Since the ordinary method of carrying on the arrangements for trade is by use of treaties, one might
expect an even higher correlation between trade treaties and trade dollar volume. However, there is one
significant factor which tends to lower the correlation in the case of the PRC. That is trade with Western States which do not recognize the PRC and which,
while willing to engage in trade, were not willing to
negotiate formal government-to-government treaties
for fear of their implication toward recognition. For
example, Canada has carried on a considerable dollar
volume of trade with the PRC and yet did not sign a
formal agreement with them until October 13, 1972.

PRC trade statistics are not precise enough to
account for the exact degree of influence that this
variable has on the overall correlation coefficient
but it is probably considerable since trade with
Western States has gradually increased to the point
of comprising nearly half of the PRC's total trade.
At the same time treaties with the Western States,
while increasing in frequency have nonetheless not
shown the dramatic increase that trade dollar volume
has shown. In spite of these factors, the correlation between overall trade treaties and trade dollar
volume is high, and if we include the Japan-type semi-
formal agreements, the correlation would probably be

even higher.

Breaking trade statistics into country groupings and individual partners proves even more productive as a behavioral indicator. In examining the Sino-Soviet treaty frequency in comparison with the Sino-Soviet trade figures, one can see that after 1960 the Soviet exports to China dropped severely as did the treaties during the same time period. A comparison of the volume of Chinese imports from the Soviet Union with the frequency of Soviet treaties for 2-year periods for 1952-1965, using the two-year projection method as above, shows a reasonably high Spearman rank order correlation, (r_S = .571). The correlation is not as high as might be expected for two reasons. The data was somewhat skewed by one two-year period and there were tied ranks in the treaty frequencies. In order to overcome this the relationship was recomputed using Pearson's product-moment correlation coefficient. A much better result was obtained (r = .719). Yet another way of displaying the relationship is to compare the percentage of Chinese imports from the Soviet Union with the percent of Soviet treaties in two-year periods for the same time frame. This yields an extremely high Spearman rank order correlation (r_S = .88).[22]

Yugoslavia presents an excellent single country

example in looking at treaty/trade correlates. Prior
to 1956 the PRC had concluded no treaties with Yugoslavia. Also during that same period (1950-1955) trade
between China and Yugoslavia had been negligible.[23]
In the period 1956-1958 the PRC concluded a total of 18
treaties with Yugoslavia. These three years represent
the highest treaty volume years, singly or in three-
year groups, between the PRC and Yugoslavia. It was
also in these three years that dollar volume of trade
reached its peak. The time lag between treaties and
trade volume is evident here though not so dramatic.
The highest treaty frequency year was 1956 and the two
highest trade years were 1956 and 1957.[24] Since 1958
treaty volume and trade have both declined.

Cuba presents another example. PRC treaties with
Cuba show a very high volume between 1961 and 1964.
Trade figures during the same time period also show
high volumes, peaking in 1965 with $213 million, the
highest trade volume year between the two countries.
After 1965 trade volume and treaty frequency both declined sharply. In the case of Cuba high treaty frequency preceded high trade volume by one year and in-
versely treaty frequency declined one year prior to the
decline in trade volume. In this case again treaties
seem to have been an excellent predictor of future
trade.

The generally high correlations between trade

data and treaty data serve again to illustrate how well
treaties mirror and predict political and economic
interactions among nation states.

Other Economic Data

Treaty frequency has proven to be a reasonably
accurate index of a country's financial status as
measured by its gross national product and its per
capita GNP. One study has shown that for all the
world's States there is an extremely high correlation
between treaty frequency and GNP, (r=.92).[25] Treaty
frequency and per capita GNP are also highly correlated (r=.58).

The People's Republic of China, however, does not
seem to reflect quite the same high correlations that
we find in the rest of the world. The PRC is the
world's second or third leading treaty maker,[26] yet
it ranks 7th in GNP among the nations of the world
and 88th in per capita GNP. Although the PRC's GNP
is relatively large its tremendous population makes
its per capita GNP among the lowest in the world.

The high treaty frequency in the case of the PRC
can be explained by the same rationale that we find
behind the motivation to be an aid donor nation. That
is primarily the PRC's drive to achieve great power
status, irrespective of internal sacrifices.

The index of GNP may also be useful in other ways.
Used in conjunction with the treaty data, compilations
of GNP for China's leading treaty partners yield some
interesting results. When correlated with treaty frequency over time, these data are a further support for
the proposition that China has attempted to form a bloc,
within the Communist bloc, of the poorer, but "ideologically purer" nations. A comparison made by Holsti
and Sullivan of treaty frequencies with per capita GNP
of the treaty partner for the periods 1949-53 and 1963-
65 indicates that during the first period "there was a
very high Spearman rank-order correlation (r_s=.79) between the number of treaties signed and the wealth of
the signatory."[27]

Results for the later period showed a marked difference (r_s=.26), thus indicating that China was perhaps
seeking out the underdeveloped nations for her treaty
relations. Carrying the investigation past the time
periods included in the Holsti and Sullivan work we
find that the correlational trend between treaty frequency and wealth of treaty partner continues to decline. Because of the high number of tied ranks in the
later treaty computations the Spearman statistic became
unusable. It was therefore necessary to recompute the
correlations using the product-moment correlation coefficient (Pearson's r).

Using two later 4-year periods, 1965-68 and 1969-

72, we find that the association between the PRC's treaty frequency and per capita GNP of her treaty partners is now a negative correlation, (r=-.24) for the 1965-68 period and (r=-.26) for the 1969-72 period Taken by themselves these particular correlations would not be considered high enough to attribute a very strong relationship between the variables. However, when viewed as a trend, we can see a constant decline from very high positive to low positive to low negative and increasingly negative correlations over time. Thus, viewed as a trend these statistics are a good representation of the direction that the PRC is pursuing in her treaty relations, i.e. toward the less-developed countries.

A further statistic was computed in support of this hypothesis. The length of time that a country had been a treaty partner with the PRC was correlated with its per capita GNP. Because of the wide divergence between these two variables and because of the wide distribution of per capita GNP a point biserial correlation was used to compute this statistic. The relationship shown was reasonably high (r_{pbis}=.496) and further supports the contention that the PRC is moving to the less wealthy States as treaty partners.

Some of this shift in treaty relations is of course accounted for by the fact that many of the poorer nations are also among the newest and could not

have signed treaties with the PRC in any earlier period. A comparison of world wide treaty trends indicates that in the later years treaties concluded by the African group of nations show a greater increase both in absolute numbers as well as percentages. From the period 1956-60 to the period 1961-65 the African group experienced a 300% increase globally in treaty volume. Most other country groupings experienced only small increases or even decreases in volume on a global scale.

While these facts do, to some extent, mitigate the trend statistics presented above for the PRC they should not be over-emphasized. First, it must be assumed that much of the increase for the African group on a world wide scale is caused by newly independent nations. Since the world wide treaty data is complete only through 1965 and since most African States became independent prior to that time it might be suspected that there would be a diminishing increase in later years, most especially after 1968. Second, among all PRC treaty partners none has gained its independence in the last period reflected in the correlations (1969-72). The last PRC treaty partner to gain independence was Equatorial Guinea in October 1968. Yet the trend has continued toward the poorer nations even in the latter period.

It can thus be concluded that while some of the
shift in direction of PRC treaty relations reflects a
natural happening in view of world wide treaty trends
caused by the recently independent States, probably
to a greater extent it reflects a purposeful effort
on the part of the PRC to assert its leadership among
these particular States.

Events Data and Treaty Frequency

During the period of Communist control over the
Chinese mainland, treaty frequency, trends and patterns have fluctuated greatly. Many of these fluctuations seem to be caused rather directly by, or
at the very least, are strongly related to, certain
events, both internal and external to the PRC. The
extent to which these changes in trends, patterns and
volume can be attributed to one category of event or
another (i.e. internal or external) should be important in determining to what extent the PRC has become a "normal" actor in the international system.

One would expect, for example, that events in
any State's external environment would (perhaps
should) have a greater effect on their treaty relations than any internal events, other than those of a
cataclysmic nature.

The reasoning behind this is simple. Given the
nature of the international system and the interre-

lated effects of the actions of the actors upon one another, States must maintain a reasonably stable appearance internationally if they are to reap the benefits of normal interactions. A fine example of this is China herself during the pre-nationalist and nationalist periods. China maintained such fine external relations that it gave the appearance to all other nations that it was extremely stable internally though this was far from the actual situation. Only when changes occur in the international environment that make it necessary for a State to shift its position are most States willing to realign their international priorities.

The unimportance of domestic events in the international system in theory is quite clear and is reflected in the widely accepted legal principle that the State continues as an international personality regardless of changes in government, as do its particular rights and obligations vis-a-vis foreign States regardless of their internal social and political systems and regimes.

Internal Events

As noted in the preceding chapter, overall PRC treaty frequency has increased at a reasonably steady rate from 1949 through 1965, with a slight downward

trend in the 1957-1960 period. This decline in treaty
frequency coincides with the Great Leap Forward and
its subsequent failure as an economic venture and China's resultant economic decline. In view of the seriously disruptive nature of the Great Leap Forward
(GLF) in China's internal affairs, one might expect
a serious decline in treaty volume, <u>unless the PRC</u>
<u>were interested in maintaining normal international</u>
<u>relations in spite of extreme internal difficulties</u>.
This appears to have been the case. The decline that
was experienced also coincides with the widening of
the Sino-Soviet split. In fact the drop in treaty
frequency for the Soviet Union and Core-Bloc countries in the 1960-61 period is nearly enough to account for the overall treaty frequency decline through
the years of the GLF and subsequent economic problems.
The implication then, is clear; an external event,
i.e. the rapidly developing Sino-Soviet split, though
not entirely unrelated to internal Chinese events,
probably did more to affect the decrease in treaty
frequency than did the internal event itself.

Only one event in PRC history stands out in its
effect on the PRC's external relations, that is the
Great Proletarian Cultural Revolution (GPCR). The Cultural Revolution in China was a cataclysmic type of
event and one which caused the PRC to alter its interna-

tional relations seriously during its tenure. Yet,
at the time of the Cultural Revolution, opinions as
to the seriousness of the event ran the full spectrum
of speculation. It was compared to the Great Leap
Forward, was it more serious? less? China's closed
door policy made it difficult for analysts to obtain
good internal indicators for their analysis. Of
necessity, a wait and see attitude was adopted by
many, others speculated.[28]

The GPCR was begun late in 1965 and was characterized by a self-imposed isolation policy by the
PRC. Treaty frequency began to show this policy
almost immediately. During 1965 treaty frequency fell
to 113 from the previous years record total of 127.
In 1966, 1967 and 1968 treaty frequency fell to 88,
44 and 38 respectively. The lowest year was 1969 with
only 26 treaties, the lowest in PRC history since 1951.
In 1966 Peking also recalled 40 ambassadors from the
46 States with which it maintained diplomatic relations.

While it is not within the scope of this study
to examine the details of the GPCR it should be noted
that this event was probably the most disruptive internal event in China since the 1949 revolution and
take over by the Communists. The rapid decline in
treaty frequency would certainly bear out this con-

clusion.

It remains, however, to discuss why the GPCR
caused the PRC to alter its external affairs while
other serious internal events, including the Great
Leap failure, did not. From 1949 up to the time of
the GPCR, the People's Republic of China had exhibited
a strong degree of "normalcy" in international relations. This was obviously the result of efforts,
despite Chinese rhetoric to the contrary, to maintain
positive and strong relations in the international
system. Yet, the Cultural Revolution caused a disruption of that normalcy. The explanation probably
lies with the fact that the Cultural Revolution was
more than simply a revolution in name only. Rather
than just "Mao's continuing revolution" it appears
to have been a genuine power struggle between suf-
ficiently diverse factions and of such magnitude as
to necessitate a temporary withdrawal from the international scene. The negative effects on foreign relations were probably exacerbated when in 1967 the
Foreign Ministry fell temporarily into the hands of a
new group of militant Maoists.[29]

It should also be noted that the retrenchment in
international relations may not be entirely without
input from prior external stimuli. In 1965 PRC foreign policy had received a series of setbacks in

Africa and Asia characterized most notably by major reversals in Ghana and Indonesia. What may have occurred then is a kind of external event-internal event interaction pattern wherein this combination in addition to the seriousness of the internal event was enough to manifest itself in the international sphere.

In 1969 and 1970 the PRC began to pull itself out of the Cultural Revolution aftermath and again turn its attention to the international environment. Treaty relations lagged about one year behind the PRC's "turn outward" but in 1970 through 1972 have shown a steady increase in volume.

External Events

There are several major external events that have affected Chinese treaty patterns since 1949. Unlike an internal event such as the Cultural Revolution, external events seem to affect direction or patterns of treaty interaction more than actual overall treaty volume.

Probably the most significant external event in PRC history prior to rapprochement with the U.S. was the Sino-Soviet dispute. The effects of the Sino-Soviet dispute can be measured in many ways only one of which is treaty patterns. One such measurement is included in a study by Holsti and Sullivan, "Chinese Actions Towards Other Nations in Various Interna-

tional Environments."[30] Holsti and Sullivan have

coded Chinese actions from 1950 through 1964. They

defined "actions," whether physical or verbal, as

anything coming from the PRC Government and crossing

their national boundaries.[31]

The data shown for the intra-bloc actions indi-

cate an increasing split between China and the Core-

Bloc countries beginning in 1962. Up until that time

the percent of positive actions had remained quite

high, the one exception being 1958. The low percent

of positive actions in that year was accounted for

by Chinese verbal attacks (i.e. negative actions) on

Yugoslavia.[32]

The very clear evidence of the Sino-Soviet dis-

pute can be seen in the declining percentage of posi-

tive actions from 1960 through 1964. The rank order

correlation between percent of positive actions and

number of Soviet treaties is reasonably high (r_s=.55).

It was shown above that similar trends were ex-

hibited by Tretiak's "level of attention to the inter-

national environment" and Chinese treaty patterns for

the same and subsequent periods.[33]

The Sino-Soviet dispute is important to PRC

treaty patterns not only because it caused the decline

in treaties between the PRC and the Soviet/Core Bloc

group but for other effects it has had on PRC treaty

patterns. For example, increasing levels of attention and increasing treaty frequency between the PRC
and Albania, two countries which otherwise seem
strange allies, is due in large part to Sino-Soviet
differences. In addition, since the rift, the PRC
has gradually turned its attention toward trade and
treaty relations with many non-Communist States. Competition with the Soviet Union has also been a partial cause for China's intense interest in the African State group.[34]

It was pointed out earlier that the Sino-Indian
border disputes had had not only a negative effect
on Sino-Indian treaty frequency but also a positive
effect on Sino-Pakistani and Sino-Nepalese treaty
relations.[35] In light of recent Soviet attention
to India, there seems little doubt that the Sino-
Soviet rift has also to some extent had its effect
on these treaty relations. There also seems little
doubt that recent Chinese aid and trade treaties with
Romania are closely tied with PRC-Soviet differences.

Another significant event and one that will undoubtedly have a great effect on PRC treaty patterns
in the future is the admission of the PRC government to the China seat in the United Nations. While
this event has not yet made a clearly defined change
in PRC treaty patterns as such, there are some dis-

cernible trends.

Since its admission to the United Nations, the PRC has concluded treaties with 11 new treaty partners, several of which are in the Western States group, including Canada. Moreover, all of these new treaty partners are U.N. members and none have become newly independent within this time frame. Thus it seems that U.N. membership itself will have a significant quasi-conservative effect on PRC treaty patterns. It would appear that the well-known political axiom about "bringing the rascals in" works as well in the case of U.N.-PRC relations.

In addition, in 1971 the PRC established diplomatic relations with an additional 17 States and in 1972, 8 more were added, bringing the total to 76 midway through 1972. There seems little doubt that there will be an eventual effect on treaty volume since the PRC has become a "legitimate" actor in the international system.

Several conclusions may be drawn about the events and their effect on PRC treaties. First, up until the present time, external events have had their greatest influence in treaty directions or patterns. In this sense the PRC appears to have settled into the international environment rather nicely. The one international event that may eventually have the greatest

effect on PRC treaty patterns is the admission to the U.N.

Up to the time of the Cultural Revolution, no internal event seemed to have any significant effect on frequency or patterns of treaties. The GPCR, however, was of such a tremendously important nature to the PRC that it disrupted not only its domestic but also its international relations significantly. In this exceptional case treaty patterns became an accurate measure of the intensity of the internal conflict. It is doubtful that the PRC will again experience an internal event of this magnitude and thus its international relations should continue to resume their normal course as Chinese treaty patterns have reflected for the past three years.

FOOTNOTES

1.   Douglas M. Johnston, "Treaty Analysis and Communist China: Preliminary Observations," Proceedings ASIL, (April 27-29, 1967) p. 127.

2.   Robert L. Price, "International Trade of Communist China, 1950-65," in An Economic Profile of Mainland China, prepared for the Joint Economic Committee Congress of the United States, New York, Praeger, 1967, p. 619.

3.   Ibid.

4.   Ibid.

5.   JMJP, February 8, 1959.

6.   JMJP, December 4, 1963 and Chou En-lai, "Report on the Work of the Government to the First Session, Third National People's Congress," December 21-22, 1964, Peking Review, (January 1, 1965) quoted in Jan S. Prybla, The Political Economy of Communist China, Scranton, Pa., International Textbook Company, 1970, p. 217

7.   SCMP, 1975:46

8.   JMJP, February 25, 1953.

9.   Prybla, op. cit., p. 222.

10.   Milton Kovner, "Communist China's Foreign Aid to Less Developed Countries," in Economic Profile, op. cit., p. 611.

11.   It is impossible to give an accurate percentage of aid to total GNP or national income, particularly for these earlier periods, as estimates for these two economic indicators vary by as much as 25%.   In addition there is the problem presented by converting 1952 Chinese yuan into U.S. dollars.   For an explanation of dual exchange rates see Robert L. Price, op. cit., p. 607.

12.   Kovner, op. cit., p. 612.

13.   Kovner, op. cit., p. 611.

14.   For a discussion of this point see Albert Feuerwerker, "Relating to the International Community,"

in Michel Oksenberg, ed., China's Developmental Experience, New York, Praeger, pp. 42-54, see esp. p. 47; See also Robert Price, op. cit., p. 583 and passim.

15.   Daniel Floyd, Mao Against Khrushchev: A Short History of the Sino-Soviet Conflict, New York, Praeger, 1964, p. 81.

16.   See Kovner, op. cit., p. 614.

17.   Ole R. Holsti and John D. Sullivan, "National-International Linkages: France and China as Non-Conforming Alliance Members," in James Rosenau, ed., Linkage Politics, New York, The Free Press, 1969, pp. 147-195.

18.   Treaty Statistics from the Treaty Information Project, University of Washington, Professor Peter H. Rohn, Director; Aid Statistics from George T. Yu, "China's Competitive Diplomacy in Africa," in Jerome A. Cohen, ed., The Dynamics of China's Foreign Relations, Harvard Asian Monograph No. 39, Cambridge, Harvard University Press, 1970, p. 77.

19.   Prybla, op. cit., p. 222.

20.   Yu, op. cit., p. 85.

21.   Ibid.

22.   Correlations contained herein are based on trade data gathered by Holsti and Sullivan through 1965 and presented in Ole R. Holsti and John D. Sullivan, op. cit., p. 147-195; and trade statistics presented in Economic Profile, op. cit., passim.

23.   Economic Profile, op. cit., p. 646.

24.   This is perhaps due to the fact that the Yugoslav trade data was adjusted for time leads and lags in shipping. See Ibid.

25.   John King Gamble, "A Correlational Model of Bilateral Treaty Frequencies," Treaty Information Project working paper #24, University of Washington, November 1970, p. 8.

26.   See supra Ch. I note 10.

27.   Holsti and Sullivan, op. cit., p. 170; Holsti and Sullivan's correlations are based on a total

246

treaty base of 1308 bilateral and multilateral treaties during the period 1949-1965.

28. For a sampling of the various analyses expressed both during and immediately after the GPCR see
for example, Philip Bridgham, "Mao's Cultural Revolution: Origin and Development," The China Quarterly, No.
29 (January-March 1967) pp.1-35; Wen-shun Chi,"The
Great Proletarian Cultural Revolution in Ideological
Perspective," Asian Survey, Vol. 9, No. 8, (August,1969)
pp. 563-579; Gene T. Hsiao, "The Background and Development of 'The Proletarian Cultural Revolution,'" Asian
Survey, Vol. 7, No.6,(June, 1967) pp. 389-404; Chalmers
Johnson, "China: The Cultural Revolution in Structure
Perspective," Asian Survey, Vol. 8,No. 1, (February,
1968) pp. 1-15; Lucian Pye, The Authority Crisis in Chi-
nese Politics, Chicago, Univ. of Chicago Press, 1967;
Ross Terrill, "The New Revolution: II [Communist China]-
The Seige Mentality," Problems of Communism, Vol. 16,
No. 2, (March-April 1967) pp. 1-10, and others in sub-
sequent volumes, Vol. 16, No. 3 (May-June, 1967)pp.1-21;
Vol. 17, No. 2, (March-April 1968) pp. 1-30; Harold M.
Vinacke, "The Continuing Chinese Revolution," Current
History, Vol. 53, No. 313 (September,1967)pp. 161-166;
Richard W. Wilson, "The Learning of Political Symbols
in Chinese Culture," Journal of Asian and African Stud-
ies, Vol. 3, Nos. 3-4 (July-October 1968) pp. 24-256;

The above cited list is not meant to be exhaustive but
merely representative of the varying approaches to the
GPCR.
29. "Background Notes: Communist China," U.S. Department of State, November, 1968.

30. Holsti and Sullivan, op. cit., pp. 169-175.

31. The New York Times Index: 1950-1964; Charles
McClelland et al, The Communist Chinese Performance in
Crisis and Non-Crisis Quantitative Studies of the Taiwan Straits Confrontation: 1950-1964, China Lake, California; Naval Ordnance Test Station, 1965; and William
H. Vatcher, Panmunjon, New York, Praeger, 1958; cited
in Holsti and Sullivan, op. cit., p. 169.

32. Holsti and Sullivan, op. cit., p. 170.

33. Daniel Tretiak, "Is China Preparing to 'Turn
Out'?: Changes in Chinese Levels of Attention to the
International Environment," Asian Survey, Vol. 11,
No. 3, (March, 1971) pp. 219-237.

34. See, George T. Yu, "China's Competitive Diplomacy in Africa," in Jerome A. Cohen, ed., The Dynamics of China's Foreign Relations, Harvard East Asian Monographs No. 39, Cambridge, Harvard University Press, 1973, pp. 69-87.

35. For a discussion of the PRC-India-Pakistan relationship, see Arthur A. Stahnke, "Diplomatic Triangle: China's Policies Toward India and Pakistan in the 1960's," in Cohen, op. cit., pp. 21-40.

CHAPTER VII

CONCLUSION

PRC Legal Theory and Practice

In terms of concern and uncertainty in the rest of the world over what type of international behavior a radically new regime might display, the PRC probably has had a greater effect on foreign expectations and speculations than any other State in the post World War II period.

Its own rhetoric, based on the doctrines of Marxism-Leninism and the Thought of Mao Tse-tung, have served little to soothe the fears of its planetary coinhabitants. It was this fear, heightened by the PRC's revolutionary rhetoric, that made other States distrust the PRC, regard it as an international outlaw and exclude it, insofar as possible, from normal international interaction patterns.

To a greater or lesser degree, all revolutionary regimes have experienced this sort of distrust and non-acceptance from the club of nation-states to which they aspire to belong. Revolutionary France, National Socialist Germany, the Soviet Union and Cuba have all experienced the difficulty of acceptance. Paradoxically, in all of these cases the actions of these nation states in the international environment did not coincide with their threatening rhetoric. The PRC

249

in this sense is no different from any of the modern
revolutionary regimes. In fact, in so far as world
interaction patterns have brought nations closer together and made it more and more difficult to act in-
dependently of each other, the PRC has found it necessary, perhaps to an even greater degree than other
revolutionary regimes, to inject itself as quickly as
possible into the mainstream of world politics.

It nonetheless considers itself a champion of a
world revolutionary struggle and thus is forced into
a position of continuing to espouse revolutionary
rhetoric but acting in a manner which will gain it
recognition as a member of the global community.

Much of the doctrine set forth by PRC writers on
international law differs rather significantly from
Western concepts of international law. As a newly
formed government, and according to their own theory,
a newly formed State, they have held extremely strict
views regarding some important facets of international
law, including one as basic as sovereignty itself.
In theory they have advanced a view of sovereignty
that would make it nearly impossible to interact
normally with other States. In practice, however,
they have consistently accepted the more realistic
view of limited sovereignty governing contemporary
international law and relations. Their participation

in treaties and international organizations is ample
evidence of this fact.

Essentially the PRC legal theory is a composite
made up of early Chinese experiences combined with
borrowed Soviet concepts and Marxist-Leninist doctrine. In total, though it is different in many ways
from the common elements in western theories of international law, it does, nonetheless, have a reasonable,
sound theoretical basis and I believe that it has been
advanced sincerely by the Chinese Communists as a logical way toward world order. It must be recognized
that the traditional and the modern views of law in
general held by the Chinese differ considerably from
Western views of law.

It has been shown in the early chapters of this
study, that the PRC often tends to apply the rules of
international law in an arbitrary fashion. This applies not only to concepts accepted by Western international law standards but to concepts peculiar to
PRC legal theory as well. However, it has also been
shown that all States tend to use international law
as a tool to serve political ends. Perhaps the only
difference between the PRC and many other States is
the Chinese assertion, based on their own revolutionary legal theory, that law is in fact a political
instrument and should be used as such.

The PRC, like other States, is not unresponsive to the fact that relations among States are based on the principle of reciprocity. Their leadership realizes that for a State to succeed in the international system it must act within a certain group of norms prescribed by the system. In spite of their rhetoric to the contrary the PRC has acted, for the most part, within the parameters of these norms.

Perhaps the most significant finding in this section of the study is that contrary to widely held beliefs, as well as contrary to their own rhetoric, the PRC is a "normal" actor insofar as other States have permitted it to be. It is among the conclusions of this study that the PRC (as well as preceding revolutionary regimes) would have conformed even more quickly to international norms if they had been given adequate incentives to do so. Paraphrasing Chairman Mao; insofar as they were kept out of the international system they were free to act as outsiders. Now, of course, with her admission to the United Nations in 1971, the PRC has become an "insider" and therefore, presumably, freedom to act otherwise is further curtailed.

PRC Treaty Practice.

The importance of treaties in PRC practice is

manifestly clear from a quantitative viewpoint alone. The 1,660 treaties included in this study place it among the world's leading treaty makers and most important actors. Even throughout most internal struggles the PRC has maintained a consistently high rate of treaty negotiations.

The PRC subscribes to the idea that treaties are among the main sources of international law. With the exception of those treaties which it considers "unequal," the PRC also subscribes to the principle of pacta sunt servanda. Most of the treaty disputes in which the PRC has been involved have been a result not of outright treaty violations, but rather of treaty interpretation. Moreover, the problem of interpretation has often been exacerbated by the mutual distrust that existed between the two partners at the time of the negotiations and the failure by both sides to come to grips with the disparities in their separate legal theories.

The PRC has relied on treaties as both a means of promoting its internal economic status and as a method for asserting its own great power status. The PRC has used aid treaties to promote trade and trade treaties to promote economic stability.

In a world of disparate legal theories and varied attitudes toward international law, the PRC has found

a common ground of security in dealing with other
nations through the formal medium of treaties. Their
refusal to enter, for a second time, into an agreement with such obscure legal force as the 1955 Agreed
Measures Announcement demonstrates that the need for
formal binding arrangements exists on both sides of
the ideological coin, and that suspicion and hope
coexist on each side in negotiating an agreement with
the other. Treaties therefore are as indispensable
to the PRC as they are to any other established State
in the international system.

Treaties as Behavioral Indicators

The PRC, as a revolutionary regime, presents
special methodological problems in an examination of
their treaty trends and patterns as indicators of international behavior and intent. The problems, however, are not of such magnitude that, with the proper caveats, they cannot be overcome and allow PRC
treaties to have the same or similar indicative and
predictive value as treaties of non-revolutionary
States.

Trade is the largest topic category among all
PRC treaties, comprising 41% of all PRC treaty dealings. This is highly indicative of the manner in
which the PRC has sought to promote economic rela-

tions throughout the world. As an overall statistic trade treaties are an accurate reflection of the PRC's dealings with other States, i.e. they are mostly interested in trade relations with other States. If, however, trade treaty volume is examined on an individual nation basis, then there tend to be disparities between trade treaty volume and actual dollar volume of trade transactions. It is the conclusion of this study that this disparity is not an abnormality caused by any practice emanating from the PRC itself, but rather is a result of the hostile political milieu in which it has been forced to operate.

From 1949 until the 1970's the United States has maintained a trade embargo against the PRC. It also refused to recognize the Communist government as the legitimate government of China. The attitudes and practices of the United States toward the PRC have also affected to a greater or lesser degree the attitudes and practices of all U.S. allies and clients toward the PRC government.

As it became increasingly evident to most capitalist nations in the world that mainland China presented a vast market for their industrial and agricultural products, economic considerations overcame political and ideological preferences. Therefore, since the mid-1960's the "Free World" States have

accounted for approximately 2/3 of China's trade. The State category called "Western Nations" in this study has accounted for nearly 50%. Yet treaty volume does not reflect this accurately.

To be sure, one can easily see that the largest category of treaties with Western States is trade (77 treaties) and that that category accounts for 75% of this State group's treaties with the PRC. What is not accurately reflected is the volume of trade with the West compared to PRC trade with all other countries. Western trade treaties account for less than 12 % of the total PRC treaties in this topic category.

The reason for this distortion is the fact that States like Canada, Australia, Japan and others have been trading with the PRC through contracts negotiated through private enterprises rather than through government to government agreements as would normally be the case. Hence, formal treaty data reflects the political facade rather than the economic fact, but if we dig only one single layer beneath the most formal surface definition of "treaty" we again find a good fit between treaties and facts.

A clarification of this dual-track pattern has already begun. Since the PRC's admission to the U.N. many nations have become formal treaty partners with

the PRC that had only heretofore carried on interactions on a semi-official basis. It is a conclusion
of this study, in the form of a prediction, that this
is the beginning of a trend and that in the future,
trade treaties will more accurately reflect trade
volume between the PRC and its various partners.

Aside from the special case of trade treaties
with Western States, all other categories of PRC
treaties seem to be accurate reflections of their
intentions in the international system. Certainly
the frequency of aid treaties to Africa, their dollar
amount of aid, (particularly viewed as a percent of
their GNP) and their rhetoric concerning the importance of the African States in the world revolutionary struggle all coincide neatly.

As a result of the comparative data used in
Chapter VI some other conclusions can be drawn about
the PRC from their treaty data. First, treaty patterns have been shown to be accurate reflections of
shifts in the international environment which directly involve the PRC. The Sino-Soviet rift caused
rather drastic shifts in PRC treaty patterns away
from the Soviet Union and its Core-Bloc countries.
Moreover, these shifts were highly correlated in degree with other indices which also reflected the
growing rift. For example, shifts toward various

forms of positive inter-bloc behavior were also reflected accurately by treaty trends.

It has been stated above that a new pattern is
developing in trade treaty relations with the Western
States. This new trend in treaty patterns directly
reflects an increasingly relaxed attitude by this set
of countries toward the PRC. On the whole then it can
be concluded that PRC treaty frequency, trends and
patterns are highly indicative and reasonably predictive of shifts in the international system as they
affect the PRC.

Treaty frequencies were also examined in regard
to Chinese domestic events. It was found that, for
the most part, the importance of maintaining normal
international relations precluded any action which
would cause a drastic change in treaty volume. This,
therefore, made treaties insensitive to most domestic
disruptions in the PRC. It was shown, however, that
events of extreme importance can be reflected in treaty volumes. The Great Proletarian Cultural Revolution
was the only internal event in the history of the PRC
to cause noticeable fluctuations in treaty frequency
that could not be explained by any external variable.
Had this fact been realized during the Cultural Revolution, outside observers could have realized the
seriousness of the event much sooner than they did,

in spite of domestic secrecy. Thus, it can be concluded that treaties, while not a sensitive indicator
of domestic events, are nonetheless accurate indicators of events of great magnitude, the seriousness of
which may not otherwise be so measurable to outside
contemporary observers.

Expectations of Future PRC Practice

Through the first 20 years of her existence the
PRC attempted to operate in an international system
of which she was not considered a legal part. In the
past few years the PRC has come increasingly to be
recognized as an important and viable member of that
system. Membership in the United Nations is certainly the benchmark of her acceptance by the other
States of the world.

Since the PRC has become a member of the United
Nations, an ever increasing number of States are ex-
tending formal recognition, establishing diplomatic
relations and entering into formal treaty relations
with this formerly ostracized State. The PRC has
long since ceased to act as a revolutionary State in
her external affairs and has carried on normal relations with a large portion of the world. Now that it
has become an accepted member of the international
community it is probable that the divergence that we

have observed in the past between revolutionary rhetoric and actual practice will diminish. The expected change should come in the direction of a soften-
ing of the hard line stand that the PRC has taken on
issues such as sovereignty, unequal treaties, subjects
of international law and international organizations.
Just as the Soviet Union began to shift its academic
and popular rhetoric to match its actions, so too
should the PRC begin to move in that direction.

A substantial body of information has been set
forth supporting the contention that China has been
attempting to establish a bloc within the Communist
system. Recent treaty patterns with Romania also
indicate that that country is growing closer to China
and further from the Soviet Union. Since the increase
in treaty frequency with Romania has come subsequent
to more friendly relations between the PRC and the
West, it is evident that the PRC will continue to
seek a position of leadership among the Communist
States while also attempting to further relations with
the Western States.

China has also been attempting to establish a
significant sphere of influence in both Sub-Saharan
Africa and non-Communist Asia. Treaty patterns in
the most recent years indicate that China has nearly
entirely recovered from the setbacks that it suffered

in these areas in the mid-1960's.

Since the People's Republic of China has taken over the Chinese seat in the United Nations they have given further indication through that body that they indeed view themselves as the champions of the underdeveloped countries. Repeatedly China has taken the part of these nations against the developed world. For example, in the 1974 United Nations Session on Raw Materials, Teng Hsiao-ping, head of the Chinese delegation made repeated verbal attacks on both the United States and the Soviet Union as "plundering" and "bullying" superpowers using "high-handed measures" to exploit the third world countries. The PRC has also taken similar stances concerning environmental controls and the law of the sea. This is not surprising in light of the recent increase in trade and aid treaties signed between China and these underdeveloped countries.

Future Research

Suggestions for future research are still limited by the availability of information concerning the PRC. This is, to some extent, being overcome in recent years, but full information is still not available to a large number of scholars. As far as this study is concerned, it would be desirable to

have treaty topics much more narrowly defined and subcategorized so that the comparability with existing
treaty information on other countries would be increased. At the present time due to the unavaila-
bility of full texts of many of the treaties, this is
not possible. It is hoped that with the PRC participation in the U.N. it will see fit to register its
treaties with that body and therefore provide a much
more reliable and comprehensive data base from which
further studies can be made.

The most exciting research prospects that suggest themselves from this study are those that arise
from the comparability between the PRC and other
revolutionary regimes that have undergone problems
of acceptance similar to those of the PRC. The question of the relationship between the unresponsiveness
of the international system to a revolutionary regime and the time lag between a revolutionary regime's beginnings and its progress toward "normality"
in its international relations is a research project
whose results would have significant pragmatic value
in world affairs and international stability.

A comprehensive comparative study of revolutionary regimes past and present and their practices in
international law would prove valuable in gaining

many answers to the problems of how to deal with revolutionary regimes as new international actors. Comparative studies could give answers to questions concerning the divergence between rhetoric and practice that might be generalized to future revolutionary regimes.

Through the use of the world wide treaty data bank of the Treaty Information Project further studies on all States can be undertaken on treaties as predictors and indicators of international behavior patterns. The treaties of the People's Republic of China, in spite of the many unusual circumstances surrounding them, have proven valuable in this respect. It should be expected that treaties for other more "normal" actors might provide an equally if not more reliable indicator of international behavior and intent. If this should prove to be the case then we would be provided with another valuable indicator with which to analyze the international system.

Appendix

TABLE 1

TREATY TOPIC CODE *

This is a hierarchical, single-entry code. One topic (and only one) has been assigned to every treaty.
These topics are grouped into eight major categories.
The first digit of each code identifies the major category, and the second digit identifies the particular
topic.

Code		Topic
IX		Diplomatic, admin. & judicial cooperation
	10	General relations & friendship & amity
	11	Frontier formalities & visas
	12	Status of refugees & stateless persons
	13	Recognition and/or estab. of new states
	14	Diplo. & consular matters & citizenship
	15	Extradition, deportation & repatriation
	16	Other judicial and/or adminis. coop.
	17	Extraterr. rights & regimes & spec.immun.
	18	Dispute settlement proc. & tribunals
	19	Other
2X		Health, educ.,culture, welfare & labor
	20	General
	21	Health, disease control at boundaries
	22	Education
	23	Culture
	24	Humanitarian & rescue,incl. war victims
	25	ILO conventions
	26	Non-ILO labor relations
	27	Research and scientific projects
	29	Other

* This table is a revised edition of the table used
in: Peter H. Rohn, "The United Nations Treaty
Series Project" International Studies Quarterly,
V. XII, No. 2, June 1968.

Topic Code (continued)

Code	Topic

3X   Trade, payments & other economic matters

30	General economic agreements
31	General trade
32	Financial, monetary, and payments
33	Foreign claims, debts and assets
34	Trade in specific commodities
35	Most-favored-nation clause
36	Double and other taxation
37	Patents and copyrights
38	Customs duties
39	Other

4X   Foreign aid and development assistance

40	General
41	Technical assistance
42	Aid
43	Loan and credit
44	U.S. Agri. Commod. Assistance Act
45	Atomic energy assistance
46	IBRD projects and loans
47	Non-IBRD development projects
49	Other

5X   Transportation and communication

50	General transportation
51	Air transport
52	Water transport
53	Land transport
54	General communications
55	Money orders and postal agreements
56	Telecommunications
57	Mass media
59	Other

Topic Code (continued)

Code	Topic

6X   Military, war and occupation

    60   General
    61   Military assistance, lend lease
    62   Military assistance missions
    63   Status & operations of forces abroad
    64   Installations, equip. and supplies
    65   Military service and citizenship
    66   War, armistice and peace
    67   War claims and reparation
    68   Occupation regime
    69   War graves and other

7X   International governmental organization

    70   General
    71   Estab. and/or constitutional change
    72   Status, privileges, and immunities
    73   Mutual relations and operations
    74   Adherence to UN Charter
    75   ICJ optional clause
    76   Trusteeship
    79   Other

8X   Ad hoc dispositions of particular matters

    80   General
    81   Specific claims or waivers
    82   Facilities and/or property
    83   Disposition of terr.& def. of frontiers
    84   Specific goods and equipment
    85   Disposal and/or conserv. of resources
    86   Control of internal finance
    89   Other

Appendix

TABLE 2

Treaty Partners by first year of treaty relations

# of new partners	Year	Treaty Partners
1	1949	North Korea
4	1950	Czechoslovakia, East Germany, Poland, U.S.S.R.
4	1951	Hungary, India, Romania, Tibet
16	1952	Belgium, Bulgaria, Ceylon, Chile, Finland, France, West Germany, Indonesia, Italy, Mongolia, Netherlands, Pakistan, Portugal, Switzerland, United Kingdom, North Vietnam
0	1953	—
2	1954	Albania, Burma
7	1955	Egypt, Japan, Lebanon, Sweden, Syria, Uruguay, U.S.A.
5	1956	Austria, Cambodia, Nepal, Sudan, Yugoslavia
2	1957	Afghanistan, Denmark
4	1958	Norway, Tunisia, UAR, Yemen
3	1959	Cuba, Guinea, Iraq
1	1960	Hong Kong
5	1961	Brazil, Ghana, Laos, Mali, Morocco
1	1962	Tanganyika
2	1963	Algeria, Somalia
6	1964	Burundi, Central African Republic, Congo (Brazzaville), Kenya, Mexico, Tanzania

Treaty partners (continued)

# of new partners	Year	Treaty Partners
1	1965	Uganda
2	1966	Malagasy, Zambia
1	1967	Mauritania
0	1968	——
1	1969	Southern Yemen
0	1970	——
4	1971	Equatorial Guinea, Ethiopia, Guyana, Peru
7	1972	Camaroon, Canada, Malta, Mauritius, Rwanda, Sierra Leone, Togo

Appendix

TABLE 3

TREATY PROFILES

On the following pages are treaty profiles for
the PRC's 20 leading treaty partners for the most
recent ten-year period considered in this study, i.e.
1963-72. Each country's profile shows the number of
treaties per year by topic category from their first
year of treaty relations with the PRC through 1972.
In addition, the upper right hand corner of each profile shows each country's rank for both the entire
period covered by the study (1949-72) and the latest
ten-year period (1963-72). Topic categories used refer to the major topic categories listed in appendix
table 1. (Supra page)

19 Treaties   **AFGHANISTAN**   rank 1949-72-23

rank 1963-72-19.5*

Topic Categories

Year	1X	2X	3X	4X	5X	6X	8X	Totals
1957	-	-	1	-	-	-	-	1
1958	-	-	-	-	-	-	-	0
1959	-	-	-	-	-	-	-	0
1960	1	-	-	-	-	-	-	1
1961	-	-	1	-	-	-	-	1
1962	-	-	1	-	-	-	-	1
1963	-	-	1	-	-	-	1	2
1964	-	-	1	-	-	-	-	1
1965	-	1	2	-	-	-	1	4
1966	-	1	2	-	-	-	-	3
1967	-	-	-	-	-	-	-	0
1968	-	-	1	-	-	-	-	1
1969	-	-	1	-	-	-	-	1
1970	-	-	-	1	-	-	-	1
1971	-	-	-	-	-	-	-	0
1972	-	-	1	-	1	-	-	2
Totals	1	2	12	1	1	0	2	19

* Indicates tied ranks.

91 Treaties   ALBANIA   Rank 1949-72 - 4
                                        Rank 1963-72 - 2

Topic Categories

Year	1X	2X	3X	4X	5X	6X	8X	Totals
1954	–	3	1	2	–	–	–	6
1955	–	2	–	–	1	–	–	3
1956	–	2	1	1	–	–	–	4
1957	–	–	1	1	1	–	–	3
1958	–	2	1	–	–	–	–	3
1959	–	–	3	1	1	–	–	5
1960	–	3	1	1	–	–	–	5
1961	1	1	1	3	1	–	–	7
1962	–	3	1	2	2	–	–	8
1963	1	2	2	1	–	–	–	6
1964	1	3	1	–	1	–	1	7
1965	–	2	3	1	1	–	–	7
1966	–	2	1	1	1	–	–	5
1967	–	1	1	1	–	–	–	3
1968	–	1	–	3	1	–	–	5
1969	–	–	–	–	–	–	–	0
1970	–	3	4	1	–	–	–	8
1971	–	1	1	1	–	–	–	3
1972	–	–	–	1	2	–	–	3
Totals	3	31	23	21	12	0	1	91

| 57 Treaties | | | | BULGARIA | | | Rank 1949-72 - 12 |
| | | | | | | | Rank 1963-72 - 13* |

Topic Categories

Year	1X	2X	3X	4X	5X	6X	8X	Totals
1952	-	1	2	-	-	-	-	3
1953	-	-	-	-	1	-	-	1
1954	-	1	2	-	-	-	-	3
1955	-	4	1	-	1	-	-	6
1956	-	2	1	-	-	-	-	3
1957	-	1	2	-	-	-	-	3
1958	-	3	2	-	-	-	-	5
1959	-	3	-	-	1	-	-	4
1960	-	2	1	-	-	-	-	3
1961	-	2	1	-	-	-	-	3
1962	-	2	1	-	-	-	-	3
1963	-	3	1	-	-	-	-	4
1964	-	3	2	-	-	-	-	5
1965	-	2	-	-	-	-	-	2
1966	-	1	1	-	-	-	-	2
1967	-	1	1	-	-	-	-	2
1968	-	-	1	-	-	-	-	1
1969	-	-	1	-	-	-	-	1
1970	-	-	1	-	-	-	-	1
1971	-	-	1	-	-	-	-	1
1972	-	-	1	-	-	-	-	1
Totals	0	31	23	0	3	0	0	57

60 Treaties   <u>CEYLON</u>   Rank 1949-72 - 11
                                            Rank 1963-72 - 5

Topic Categories

Year	1X	2X	3X	4X	5X	6X	8X	Totals
1952	–	–	4	–	–	–	–	4
1953	–	–	1	–	–	–	–	1
1954	–	–	1	–	–	–	–	1
1955	–	–	3	–	–	–	–	3
1956	–	–	1	–	–	–	–	1
1957	–	–	4	1	–	–	–	5
1958	–	–	–	1	–	–	–	1
1959	–	–	2	1	–	–	–	3
1960	–	–	2	–	–	–	–	2
1961	–	–	3	1	–	–	–	4
1962	1	–	4	–	–	–	–	5
1963	–	–	1	–	1	–	–	2
1964	–	–	4	4	–	–	–	8
1965	–	–	3	1	–	–	–	4
1966	–	–	3	–	–	–	–	3
1967	–	–	2	–	–	–	–	2
1968	–	–	–	–	–	–	–	0
1969	–	–	2	–	–	–	–	2
1970	–	–	–	2	–	–	–	2
1971	–	–	1	1	1	–	–	3
1972	–	–	2	1	1	–	–	4
Totals	1	0	43	13	3	0	0	60

15 Treaties   CONGO   (Brazzaville)

Rank 1949-72 - 29
Rank 1963-72 - 19.5*

Topic Categories

Year	1X	2X	3X	4X	5X	6X	8X	Totals
1964	1	1	2	1	1	-	-	6
1965	-	1	2	1	-	-	-	4
1966	-	1	-	-	-	-	-	1
1967	-	-	-	-	-	-	-	0
1968	-	-	-	-	-	-	-	0
1969	-	-	1	1	-	-	-	2
1970	-	1	-	-	-	-	-	1
1971	-	-	-	1	-	-	-	1
1972	-	-	-	-	-	-	-	0
Totals	1	4	5	4	1	-	-	15

40 Treaties   <u>CUBA</u>   Rank 1949-72 - 13
                                          Rank 1963-72 - 10*

Topic Categories

Year	1X	2X	3X	4X	5X	6X	8X	Totals
1959	-	-	1	-	-	-	-	1
1960	-	2	2	1	-	-	-	5
1961	-	2	3	-	4	-	-	9
1962	-	1	1	-	2	-	-	4
1963	-	2	2	1	-	-	-	5
1964	-	1	3	-	1	-	-	5
1965	-	2	-	-	-	-	-	2
1966	-	1	1	-	-	-	-	2
1967	-	-	1	-	-	-	-	1
1968	-	-	-	-	-	-	-	0
1969	-	-	1	-	-	-	-	1
1970	-	-	1	-	-	-	-	1
1971	-	-	3	-	-	-	-	3
1972	-	-	1	-	-	-	-	1
Totals	0	11	20	2	7	0	0	40

73 Treaties   CZECHOSLOVAKIA
                   Rank 1949-72 - 7.5*
                   Rank 1963-72 - 13*

Topic Categories

Year	1X	2X	3X	4X	5X	6X	8X	Totals
1950	-	-	1	-	-	-	-	1
1951	-	-	1	-	-	-	-	1
1952	-	2	-	-	3	-	-	5
1953	-	2	1	-	1	-	-	4
1954	-	2	1	-	-	-	-	3
1955	-	2	3	-	-	-	-	5
1956	-	4	1	-	-	-	-	5
1957	1	3	1	-	-	-	-	5
1958	-	2	2	-	-	-	-	4
1959	-	4	2	-	1	-	-	7
1960	1	2	1	-	-	-	-	4
1961	-	3	1	-	-	-	-	4
1962	-	3	2	-	-	-	-	5
1963	-	2	2	-	-	-	-	4
1964	-	2	1	-	-	-	-	3
1965	-	4	1	-	-	-	-	5
1966	-	2	1	-	-	-	-	3
1967	-	-	-	-	-	-	-	0
1968	-	-	1	-	-	-	-	1
1969	-	-	1	-	-	-	-	1
1970	-	-	1	-	-	-	-	1
1971	-	-	1	-	-	-	-	1
1972	-	-	1	-	-	-	-	1
Totals	2	39	27	0	5	0	0	73

73 Treaties   <u>EAST GERMANY</u>

Rank 1949-72 - 7.5*
Rank 1963-72 -10 *

Year	Topic Categories							Total
	1X	2X	3X	4X	5X	6X	8X	
1950	-	-	1	-	-	-	-	1
1951	-	1	-	-	2	-	-	3
1952	-	-	1	-	-	-	-	1
1953	-	3	2	-	1	-	-	6
1954	-	3	1	-	1	-	-	5
1955	1	3	3	-	-	-	-	7
1956	-	2	1	-	-	-	-	3
1957	-	3	1	-	-	-	1	5
1958	-	2	3	-	-	-	-	5
1959	1	2	1	1	2	-	-	7
1960	1	2	2	-	-	-	-	5
1961	-	1	2	-	-	-	-	3
1962	-	2	1	-	-	-	-	3
1963	-	2	1	-	-	-	-	3
1964	-	3	1	-	-	-	-	4
1965	-	2	1	-	-	-	-	3
1966	-	2	1	-	-	-	-	3
1967	-	-	1	-	-	-	-	1
1968	-	-	1	-	-	-	-	1
1969	-	-	1	-	-	-	-	1
1970	-	-	1	-	-	-	-	1
1971	-	-	1	-	-	-	-	1
1972	-	-	1	-	-	-	-	1
Totals	3	33	29	1	6	0	1	73

38 Treaties   <u>GUINEA</u>

Rank 1949-72 - 14
Rank 1963-72 - 7

| Year | Topic Categories | | | | | | | Total |
	1X	2X	3X	4X	5X	6X	8X	
1959	-	2	-	-	-	-	-	2
1960	1	1	1	1	-	-	-	4
1961	-	1	-	1	-	-	-	2
1962	-	1	1	-	1	-	-	3
1963	-	-	1	-	-	-	-	1
1964	-	2	1	-	2	-	-	5
1965	-	2	-	-	2	-	-	4
1966	-	2	3	2	-	-	-	7
1967	-	-	-	-	-	-	-	0
1968	-	-	1	1	-	-	-	2
1969	-	-	2	1	-	-	-	3
1970	-	1	2	-	-	-	-	3
1971	-	-	1	-	-	-	-	1
1972	-	-	1	-	-	-	-	1
Totals	1	12	14	6	5	0	0	38

63 Treaties   <u>HUNGARY</u>   Rank 1949-72 - 9
Rank 1963-72 - 17

Topic Categories

Year	1X	2X	3X	4X	5X	6X	8X	Total
1951	-	1	1	-	-	-	-	2
1952	-	1	-	-	-	-	-	1
1953	-	2	1	-	3	-	-	6
1954	-	2	-	-	-	-	-	2
1955	-	2	1	-	-	-	-	3
1956	-	2	1	-	-	-	-	3
1957	-	2	1	1	-	-	-	4
1958	1	2	4	-	-	-	-	7
1959	1	4	1	-	2	-	-	8
1960	-	2	1	-	-	-	-	3
1961	-	2	2	-	-	-	-	4
1962	-	2	1	-	-	-	-	3
1963	-	2	1	-	-	-	-	3
1964	-	1	1	-	1	-	-	3
1965	-	2	1	-	-	-	-	3
1966	-	1	1	-	-	-	-	2
1967	-	-	1	-	-	-	-	1
1968	-	-	1	-	-	-	-	1
1969	-	-	1	-	-	-	-	1
1970	-	-	1	-	-	-	-	1
1971	-	-	1	-	-	-	-	1
1972	-	-	1	-	-	-	-	1
Totals	2	30	24	1	6	0	0	63

117 Treaties   NORTH KOREA   Rank 1949-72 - 3
                                       Rank 1963-72 - 3

Topic Categories

Year	1X	2X	3X	4X	5X	6X	8X	Totals
1949	–	–	–	–	3	–	–	3
1950	–	–	1	–	–	–	–	1
1951	–	–	–	–	–	–	–	0
1952	–	–	–	–	–	–	–	0
1953	–	–	1	–	–	–	–	1
1954	–	–	6	1	2	–	–	9
1955	–	3	1	–	–	–	–	4
1956	–	1	1	1	1	–	2	6
1957	–	4	2	2	2	–	–	10
1958	–	1	6	2	–	–	2	11
1959	–	2	–	–	2	–	1	5
1960	–	4	1	2	1	–	–	8
1961	1	2	1	2	–	–	–	6
1962	1	3	3	–	–	–	–	7
1963	–	3	1	–	1	–	1	6
1964	–	3	1	1	3	–	–	8
1965	–	3	2	–	2	–	–	7
1966	–	4	1	–	1	–	–	6
1967	–	2	–	–	–	–	–	2
1968	–	–	1	–	–	–	–	1
1969	–	–	1	–	–	–	–	1
1970	–	1	2	1	–	–	–	4
1971	–	3	2	–	2	1	–	8
1972	–	1	1	–	–	–	1	3
Totals	2	40	35	12	20	1	7	117

25 Treaties   <u>MALI</u>   Rank 1949-72 - 21
Rank 1963-72 - 15.5*

Topic Categories

Year	1X	2X	3X	4X	5X	6X	8X	Total
1961	-	1	1	2	-	-	-	4
1962	-	2	1	-	-	-	-	3
1963	-	4	-	1	1	-	-	6
1964	1	2	-	1	-	-	-	4
1965	-	1	-	1	-	-	1	3
1966	-	1	-	1	-	-	-	2
1967	-	-	-	1	-	-	-	1
1968	-	-	-	1	-	-	-	1
1969	-	-	-	-	-	-	-	0
1970	-	-	1	-	-	-	-	1
1971	-	-	-	-	-	-	-	0
1972	-	-	-	-	-	-	-	0
Totals	1	11	3	8	1	0	1	25

62 Treaties   <u>MONGOLIA</u>   Rank 1949-72 - 10
Rank 1963-72 - 15.5*

Topic Categories

Year	1X	2X	3X	4X	5X	6X	8X	Totals
1952	-	-	1	-	-	-	-	1
1953	-	-	2	1	2	-	-	5
1954	-	1	2	-	-	-	-	3
1955	-	1	-	-	2	-	-	3
1956	-	-	2	1	1	-	-	4
1957	-	1	-	-	1	-	-	2
1958	-	2	1	1	3	-	-	7
1959	-	1	2	-	-	-	-	3
1960	1	2	1	2	1	-	-	7
1961	1	1	1	1	1	-	-	5
1962	-	2	1	-	-	-	1	4
1963	-	1	1	-	-	-	-	2
1964	-	3	1	-	-	-	1	5
1965	-	1	1	-	-	-	-	2
1966	-	2	1	-	-	-	-	3
1967	-	-	-	-	-	-	-	0
1968	-	-	1	-	-	-	-	1
1969	-	-	1	-	-	-	-	1
1970	-	-	1	-	-	-	-	1
1971	-	-	1	-	-	-	-	1
1972	-	-	2	-	-	-	-	2
Totals	2	18	23	6	11	0	2	62

37 Treaties   <u>NEPAL</u>   Rank 1949-72 - 15
                                           Rank 1963-72 - 8

Topic Categories

Year	1X	2X	3X	4X	5X	6X	8X	Total
1956	3	-	2	1	-	-	-	6
1957	-	-	-	-	-	-	-	0
1958	-	-	-	-	-	-	-	0
1959	-	-	-	-	-	-	-	0
1960	1	-	-	1	-	-	1	3
1961	-	1	-	2	-	-	1	4
1962	1	-	-	-	-	-	-	1
1963	-	-	-	-	1	-	1	2
1964	1	1	1	-	-	-	1	4
1965	-	1	-	1	1	-	-	3
1966	-	-	2	1	-	-	-	3
1967	-	-	-	3	-	-	-	3
1968	-	1	2	1	-	-	-	4
1969	-	-	-	-	-	-	-	0
1970	-	-	-	-	-	-	-	0
1971	-	-	-	1	-	-	2	3
1972	-	-	1	-	-	-	-	1
Totals	6	4	8	11	2	0	6	37

34 Treaties   PAKISTAN Rank 1949-72 - 17
               Rank 1963-72 - 6

Topic Categories

Year	1X	2X	3X	4X	5X	6X	8X	Total
1952	-	-	1	-	-	-	-	1
1953	-	-	1	-	-	-	-	1
1954	-	-	-	-	-	-	-	0
1955	-	-	-	-	-	-	-	0
1956	-	-	1	-	-	-	-	1
1957	-	-	-	-	-	-	-	0
1958	-	-	3	-	-	-	-	3
1959	-	-	-	-	-	-	-	0
1960	-	-	-	-	-	-	-	0
1961	-	-	-	-	-	-	-	0
1962	-	-	-	-	-	-	-	0
1963	-	-	2	-	3	-	1	6
1964	-	-	-	-	2	-	-	2
1965	-	1	-	2	-	-	1	4
1966	-	1	1	1	1	-	-	4
1967	-	2	1	1	-	-	-	4
1968	-	-	2	-	-	-	-	2
1969	-	-	-	-	-	-	-	0
1970	-	-	3	-	-	-	-	3
1971	-	-	1	-	-	-	-	1
1972	-	-	2	-	-	-	-	2
Totals	0	4	18	4	6	0	2	34

78 Treaties   POLAND   Rank 1949-72 - 5
                                     Rank 1963-72 - 10*

Topic Categories

Year	1X	2X	3X	4X	5X	6X	8X	Totals
1950	-	-	1	-	-	-	-	1
1951	-	1	1	-	4	-	1	7
1952	-	1	-	-	-	-	-	1
1953	-	1	1	-	1	-	-	3
1954	-	2	1	-	-	-	-	3
1955	-	2	2	-	-	-	-	4
1956	-	5	1	-	2	-	-	8
1957	-	5	1	-	-	-	-	6
1958	-	1	3	-	-	-	-	4
1959	-	3	2	-	1	-	-	6
1960	-	4	2	-	-	-	-	6
1961	-	1	3	-	-	-	-	4
1962	-	3	1	-	-	-	-	4
1963	-	2	1	-	-	-	-	3
1964	-	3	1	-	-	-	-	4
1965	-	3	1	-	-	-	-	4
1966	-	2	1	-	-	-	-	3
1967	-	1	1	-	-	-	-	2
1968	-	-	1	-	-	-	-	1
1969	-	-	1	-	-	-	-	1
1970	-	-	1	-	-	-	-	1
1971	-	-	1	-	-	-	-	1
1972	-	-	1	-	-	-	-	1
Totals	0	40	29	0	8	0	1	78

74 Treaties   <u>ROMANIA</u>   Rank 1949-72 - 6
                                           Rank 1963-72 - 4

Year	Topic Categories							Totals
	1X	2X	3X	4X	5X	6X	8X	
1951	–	1	–	–	–	–	–	1
1952	–	–	1	–	–	–	–	1
1953	–	3	1	–	1	–	–	5
1954	–	3	1	–	1	–	–	5
1955	–	2	1	–	1	–	–	4
1956	–	2	1	–	–	–	–	3
1957	–	2	1	–	–	–	–	3
1958	–	1	2	–	1	–	–	4
1959	–	3	2	–	–	–	–	5
1960	–	2	1	–	–	–	–	3
1961	–	2	1	–	–	–	–	3
1962	–	2	1	–	–	–	–	3
1963	–	3	2	–	–	–	–	5
1964	–	2	1	–	1	–	–	4
1965	–	3	1	–	–	–	–	4
1966	–	2	–	–	–	–	–	2
1967	–	2	2	–	–	–	–	4
1968	–	–	–	–	–	–	–	0
1969	–	–	1	–	–	–	–	1
1970	–	1	1	2	–	–	–	4
1971	–	–	3	4	–	–	–	7
1972	–	1	–	–	2	–	–	3
Totals	0	37	24	6	7	0	0	74

16 Treaties   **TANZANIA**   Rank 1949-72 - 27.5*
     Rank 1963-72 - 18

Topic Categories

Year	1X	2X	3X	4X	5X	6X	8X	Total
1964	-	-	1	-	-	-	-	1
1965	1	-	3	1	-	-	-	5
1966	-	1	1	1	1	-	-	4
1967	-	-	-	-	-	-	-	0
1968	-	-	-	6	-	-	-	6
1969	-	-	-	-	-	-	-	0
1970	-	-	-	-	-	-	-	0
1971	-	-	-	-	-	-	-	0
1972	-	-	-	-	-	-	-	0
Totals	1	1	5	8	1	0	0	16

141 Treaties Topic Categories				U.S.S.R.			Rank 1949-72 - 1 Rank 1963-72 - 13*	
Year	1X	2X	3X	4X	5X	6X	8X	Totals
1950	3	2	2	2	2	–	8	19
1951	–	–	1	1	3	–	2	7
1952	–	1	2	1	–	1	–	5
1953	–	–	–	2	–	–	2	4
1954	–	3	1	3	2	–	4	13
1955	–	1	4	2	–	–	–	7
1956	–	4	1	1	2	–	2	10
1957	–	5	3	–	4	–	1	13
1958	–	3	2	2	–	–	–	7
1959	2	6	2	2	–	–	–	12
1960	–	3	1	–	1	–	1	6
1961	–	6	5	–	1	–	–	12
1962	1	3	1	–	1	–	–	6
1963	–	3	1	–	1	–	–	5
1964	–	1	2	–	–	–	–	3
1965	–	3	1	–	–	–	–	4
1966	–	2	1	–	1	–	–	4
1967	–	–	1	–	–	–	–	1
1968	–	–	–	–	–	–	–	0
1969	–	–	–	–	–	–	–	0
1970	–	–	1	–	–	–	–	1
1971	–	–	1	–	–	–	–	1
1972	–	–	1	–	–	–	–	1
Totals	6	46	34	16	18	1	20	141

121 Treaties   **NORTH VIETNAM**   Rank 1949-72 - 2

Topic Categories   Rank 1963-72 - 1

Year	1X	2X	3X	4X	5X	6X	8X	Total
1952	-	-	-	-	1	-	-	1
1953	-	-	1	-	-	-	-	1
1954	-	-	3	5	2	-	-	10
1955	-	2	6	1	1	-	-	10
1956	-	-	2	2	2	-	-	6
1957	-	3	2	1	-	-	-	6
1958	-	-	1	2	2	-	-	5
1959	-	3	3	2	-	-	-	8
1960	-	3	3	2	-	-	-	8
1961	-	2	1	2	1	-	-	6
1962	1	3	2	-	-	-	1	7
1963	-	1	1	-	1	-	1	4
1964	-	3	1	-	4	-	-	8
1965	-	4	1	2	-	-	-	7
1966	-	4	1	2	1	-	-	8
1967	-	2	1	1	-	-	-	4
1968	-	-	1	1	1	-	-	3
1969	-	-	1	1	-	-	-	2
1970	-	2	1	5	-	1	-	9
1971	-	1	1	3	1	-	-	6
1972	-	-	-	1	-	1	-	2
Totals	1	33	33	33	17	2	2	121

BIBLIOGRAPHY

English Language Sources

Adams, L. Jerold, Theory, Law and Policy of Contemporary Japanese Treaties, Dobbs Ferry, New York, Oceana, 1974.

_____, "Japanese Treaty Patterns," Asian Survey, Vol. 12, No. 3 (March, 1972) pp.242-258.

Ambekar, G.V. and Divekar, V.D., eds., Documents on China's Relations with South and Southeast Asia (1949-1962), Bombay, Allied, 1964.

Barnett, A. Doak, Communist China and Asia, New York, Vintage, 1960.

Blaustein, A.P., ed., Fundamental Legal Documents of Communist China, South Hackensack, N.J., Rothman, 1962.

Bishop, William, International Law, 3rd ed., Boston, Little, Brown and Co., 1971.

Bokor-Szego, Hanna, New States and International Law, Budapest, Akademiai Kiado, 1970.

Bot, Bernard R., Nonrecognition and Treaty Relations, Leyden, A.W. Sijthoff, 1968.

Bowett, D.W., The Law of the Sea, Dobbs Ferry, New York, Oceana, 1967.

Bridgham, Philip, "Mao's Cultural Revolution, Origin and Development," The China Quarterly, No. 29, (January-March, 1967).

Brierly, James L., The Law of Nations, London, Oxford Press, 1936.

Briggs, Herbert, The Law of Nations, New York, F.S. Crofts, 1938.

Brownlie, I., Principles of Public International Law, London, Oxford University Press, 1966.

Chen, Theodore H.E., ed., The Chinese Communist Regime: Documents and Commentary, New York, Praeger, 1967.

Cheng Tao, "Communist China and the Law of the Sea," American Journal of International Law, Vol. 63, No. 1, 1969.

'Chinese Government Statement: China's Aid to Vietnam in Fighting U.S. Aggression Further Ceases to be Subject to Any Bounds or Restrictions," Peking Review,Vol. 9, No. 28, (July 8, 1966) pp. 19-20.

Chiu, Hungdah, The Capacity of International Organizations to Conclude Treaties and the Special Legal Aspects of the Treaties so Concluded, The Hague, Martinus Nijhoff, 1966.

_____, The People's Republic of China and the Law of Treaties, Cambridge, Mass., Harvard University Press, 1972.

_____, "Certain Legal Aspects of Communist China's Treaty Practice," Proceedings of the American Society of International Law, Sixty-First Annual Meeting, 1967.

_____, "Communist China's Attitude Toward International Law," American Journal of International Law, Vol. 60, No. 1, 1966.

_____, "The Development of Chinese International Law Terms and The Problem of Their Translation into English," Journal of Asian Studies, Vol. 27, 1968, p. 485.

_____, "Suspension and Termination of Treaties in Communist China's Theory and Practice," Osteuropa-Recht, Vol. 15, 1969.

Christol, Carl Q. "Communist China and International Law - Strategy and Tactics," Western Political Science Quarterly, Vol. 21, 1958.

Chua, Ivy Leng-Eng, "Communist China and International Law," The Quarterly Journal of the Library of Congress, Vol. 24, 1967.

Clubb, O. Edmund and Seligman, Eustace, The International Position of Communist China, Dobbs Ferry, N. Y., Oceana, 1965.

Clyde, Paul H., The Far East: A History of the Impact of the West on Eastern Asia, New York, Prentice-Hall, 1948.

Cohen, Jerome A., The Criminal Process in the People's Republic of China: 1949-1963, Cambridge, Mass., Harvard University Press, 1968.

_____, People's China and International Law: A Documentary Study, Princeton, New Jersey, Princeton University Press, 1974.

_____, ed.,China's Practice of International Law: Some Case Studies, Cambridge, Mass., Harvard University Press, 1972.

_____, ed., The Dynamics of China's Foreign Relations, Harvard Asian Monographs #39, Cambridge, Mass., Harvard University Press, 1970.

_____, "Chinese Attitudes Toward International Law, And Our Own," Proceedings of the American Society of International Law, Sixty-First Annual Meeting, 1967.

Confucius, The Great Learning, Ch. 1, (E. Pound translation, 1939)

Constitution of the People's Republic of China, Peking , Foreign Languages Press, 1955.

Current Background, Hong Kong, U.S. Consulate Hong Kong, 1950-

"Declaration on China's Territorial Sea," Peking Review, Vol. 1, No. 28, (September 9, 1958) p.21.

De Muralt, R.W.G., The Problem of State Succession with Regard to Treaties, The Hague, W.P. Van Stockum and Zoom, 1954.

Department of State, The Conduct of Communist China, Washington, D.C., U.S. Government Printing Office, 1963.

Department of State Bulletin, "U.S., Red China Announce Measures for Return of Civilians" No. 847, Sept. 19, 1955.

Directory and Chronicle for China, Japan, Korea, etc., Hong Kong, Hong Kong Daily Press, 1940.

Dulles, John F., "Challenge for Peace in the Far East" Department of State Bulletin, No. 39. 1958.

Edwards, Randle R., "The Attitude of the People's Re-
     public of China Toward International Law and the
     United Nations," Papers on China, Vol. 17, 1963.

Falk, Richard, "Alwyn V. Freeman vs. Myres S. McDougal"
     American Journal of International Law, V. 59, no.
     1 (January, 1965).

Feuerwerker, Albert, "Relating to the International
     Community" in Michel Oksenberg, China's Develop-
     mental Experience, New York, Praeger, 1973.

Fishel, Wesley R., The End of Extraterritoriality in
     China, Berkeley, University of California Press,
     1952.

Floyd, Daniel, Mao Against Khrushchev: A Short History
     of the Sino-Soviet Conflict, New York, Praeger,
     1964.

Friedmann, Wolfgang, Lissitzyn, Oliver and Pugh, Richard
     C., eds., International Law Cases and Materials,
     St. Paul, West, 1969.

Gamble, John King, "A Correlational Model of Bilateral
     Treaty Frequencies," Treaty Information Project
     Working Paper #24, University of Washington,
     November 1970.

Ghana Ministry of Information, Nkrumah's Subversion
     in Africa, Accra-Tema, Ghana, 1966.

Ginsburgs, George, Communist China and Tibet, The First
     Dozen Years, The Hague, Martinus Nijhoff, 1964.

Gittings, John, Survey of the Sino-Soviet Dispute, New
     York and London, Oxford University Press, 1968.

Green, L.C., "Legal Aspects of the Sino-Indian Border
     Dispute," The China Quarterly, No. 3, (July-
     September, 1960).

Grotius, H., De jure belli ac pacis, (On the Law of
     War and Peace), Translated by F.W. Kelsey from
     1646 ed., Vol. II., Washington D.C., Carnegie
     Endowment for International Peace, 1925.

Halperin, Morton, "Is China Turning In?" Harvard Uni-
     versity Center for International Affairs, No. 12,
     (December, 1965).

Hinton, Harold C., Communist China in World Politics, Boston, Houghton Mifflin, 1966.

Holloway, Kaye, Modern Trends in Treaty Law, London, Stevens and Sons, 1967.

Holsti, Ole R. and Sullivan, John D., "National and International Linkages: France and China as Non-Conforming Alliance Members," in James Rosenau, ed., Linkage Politics, New York, The Free Press, 1969.

Hoyt, Edwin C., National Policy and International Law: Case Studies from American Canal Policy, Monograph Series in World Affairs, Vol. 4, No. 1, Denver, Denver University Press, 1966-67.

_____, The Unanimity Rule in the Revision of Treaties, The Hague, Martinus Nijhoff, 1959.

Hsia Tao-tai, Guide to Selected Legal Sources of Mainland China, Washington, D. C., Library of Congress, 1967.

Hsiao, Gene T., "The Background and Development of 'The Proletarian Cultural Revolution'" Asian Survey, Vol. 7, No. 6 (June, 1967)

_____, "Communist China's Foreign Trade Contracts and Means of Settling Disputes," Vanderbilt Law Review, Vol. 22, 1969.

_____, "Communist China's Foreign Trade Organization," Vanderbilt Law Review, Vol. 21, 1968.

_____, "Communist China's Trade Treaties and Agreements," Vanderbilt Law Review, Vol. 20, 1968.

Hsiung, James Chieh, Law and Policy in China's Foreign Relations, New York, Columbia University Press, 1972.

Jan, George P., "Japan's Trade with Communist China," Asian Survey, Vol. 9, No. 12, (December, 1969).

Johnson, Chalmers, "China: The Cultural Revolution in Structure Perspective," Asian Survey, Vol. 8, No. 1 (February, 1968).

Johnston, Douglas M., "Treaty Analysis and Communist China: Preliminary Observations," Proceedings of the American Society of International Law, Sixty-First Annual Meeting, 1967.

Johnston, Douglas M., and Chiu, Hungdah, Agreements of the People's Republic of China, 1949-1967: A Calendar, Cambridge, Mass., Harvard University Press, 1968.

Joint Economic Committee Congress of the United States, An Economic Profile of Mainland China, 2 Vols., Washington, D. C., U.S. Government Printing Office, 1967.

Kozhevnikov, F.I., International Law, Moscow, Foreign Languages Publishing House, n.d.

Lall, Arthur, How Communist China Negotiates, New York, Columbia University Press, 1968.

Lee, Luke T., China and International Agreements: A Study of Compliance, Durham, N.C., Rule of Law Press, 1969.

_____, "Treaty Relations of the People's Republic of China: A Study of Compliance," University of Pennsylvania Law Review, Vol. 116, 1969.

Leech, Noyes E., Oliver, Covey T., and Sweeney, Joseph M., The International Legal System, Mineola, New York, Foundation Press, 1973.

Lejnieks, Juris A., "The Nomenclature of Treaties: A Quantitative Analysis," The Texas International Law Forum, Vol. II, No. 2, 1966.

Leng, Shao Chuan and Chiu, Hungdah, Law in Chinese Foreign Policy: Communist China and Selected Problems in International Law, Dobbs Ferry, N. Y., Oceana, 1972.

Li, Victor H., "Legal Aspects of Trade with Communist China," Columbia Journal of Transnational Law, Vol. 3, 1964.

Lissitzyn, Oliver J., "Treaties and Changed Circumstances (Rebus sic stantibus)" American Journal of International Law, Vol. 61, No. 4,(October, 1967).

Logoreci, Anton, "Albania and China: The Incongruous Alliance," Current History, Vol. 52, No. 308, (April, 1967).

Lowenthal, Richard and Brzezinski, Zbigniew, eds.,
    Africa and the Communist World, Stanford, Stan-
    ford University Press, 1963.

McClelland, Charles, et al., The Communist Chinese
    Performance in Crisis and Non-Crisis: Quantita-
    tive Studies on the Taiwan Straits Confrontation:
    1950-1964, China Lake, California, Naval Ordnance
    Test Station, 1965.

McDougal, Myres S., Laswell, Harold D., and Miller,
    James C., The Interpretation of Agreements and
    World Public Order, New Haven, Yale University
    Press, 1967.

Morse, Hosea Ballou, The International Relations of
    the Chinese Empire, Vol. I., London, Longmans,
    Green and Co., 1910.

"A New Peak in the Militant Friendship of the Chinese
    and Albanian Peoples", China Reconstructs,
    Peking, Vol. 18, No. 1, (January, 1969).

North, Robert, The Foreign Relations of China, Bel-
    mont, California, Dickenson, 1969.

O'Connell, D.P., International Law, Vol. I, London,
    Stevens, 1965.

Oksenberg, Michel, China's Developmental Experience,
    New York, Praeger, 1973.

Oppenheim, L., International Law, Vol. 1, 8th ed.,
    Lauterpacht, London, Longmans, Green & Co., 1955.

Price, Robert L., "International Trade of Communist
    China, 1950-65" in An Economic Profile of Main-
    land China prepared for the Joint Economic Com-
    mittee Congress of the U. S., New York, Praeger,
    1967.

Prybla, Jan S., The Political Economy of Communist
    China, Scranton, Pa., International Textbook Co.,
    1970.

Pufendorf, Samuel, De jure naturae et gentium, (On
    the Law of Nature and Nations), Vol. II, Trans-
    lated by C.H. Oldfather and W.A. Oldfather from
    1688 ed., Washington D. C., Carnegie Endowment
    for International Peace, 1934.

Putney, Albert H., "The Termination of Unequal Treaties," Proceedings of the American Society of International Law, Twenty-First Annual Meeting, 1927.

Pye, Lucian, The Authority Crisis in Chinese Politics, Chicago, University of Chicago Press, 1967.

"Refuting U.S. State Department: Chinese Statement on the Question of Exchanging Correspondents between China and the U.S.," Peking Review, Vol. 3, No. 29, (September 14, 1960).

Reithel, Curtis G., "A Quantitative Analysis of Treaties Entering into Force Upon Signature," Treaty Information Project working paper #36, University of Washington, 1970.

Rohn, Peter H.,"Canada in the United Nations Treaty Series: A Global Perspective," Canadian Yearbook of International Law, 1966.

_____, "A Computer Search in Soviet Treaties," International Lawyer, Vol. 2, No. 4, (July, 1968).

_____, "Institutionalism in the Law of Treaties: A Case of Combining Teaching and Research," American Society of International Law Proceedings, 1965.

_____, "Turkish Treaties in Global Perspective," Turkish Yearbook of International Law, 1965,

_____, "The United Nations Treaty Series Project," International Studies Quarterly, Vol. XII, (June, 1968).

Roucek, Joseph S., "Nepal on a Tight Rope," Eastern World, Vol. 21, No. 5/6, (May/June, 1967).

Rosenne, Shabtai, The Law of Treaties, Dobbs Ferry, N. Y., Oceana, 1970.

Rubin, Alfred P., "The Position of Tibet in International Law," China Quarterly, No. 35 (July-September, 1968).

Scheinman, Lawrence and Wilkinson, David, International Law and Political Crisis, Boston, Little, Brown, 1968.

Schurman, Franz., Ideology and Organization in Communist China, Berkeley, University of California Press, 1969.

Schwarzenberger, Georg, A Manual of International Law, 5th ed., New York, Praeger, 1967.

Scott, Gary L., "Treaties of the People's Republic of China: A Quantitative Analysis," Asian Survey, Vol. 13, No. 5, (May, 1973).

Simon, Sheldon W., The Broken Triangle: Peking, Djakarta and the PKI, Baltimore, Johns Hopkins Press, 1969.

The Sino-Indian Boundary Question, Peking, Foreign Languages Press, 1962.

Slusser, Robert and Triska, Jan, A Calendar of Soviet Treaties, 1917-1957, Stanford, Stanford University Press, 1959.

Steiner, H. Arthur, "The Mainsprings of Chinese Communist Foreign Policy," American Journal of International Law, Vol. 54, No. 1, (January, 1950).

Subcommittee for National Security and International Operations, Problems of Negotiation with Communist China, Washington D. C., U. S. Government Printing Office, February, 1969.

Syatauw, J.J.G., Some Newly Established Asian States and the Development of International Law, The Hague, Martinus Nijhoff, 1961.

Tretiak, Daniel, "Is China Preparing to 'Turn Out'?: Changes in Chinese Levels of Attention to the International Environment," Asian Survey, Vol. XI, No. 3, (March, 1971).

_____,"Peking's Policy Toward Sinkiang: Trouble on the New Frontier," Current Scene, Hong Kong, Vol. 24, No. 11, (November 15, 1963).

Triska, Jan F., "Soviet Treaty Law: A Quantitative Analysis," Law and Contemporary Problems, Vol. 29, No. 3.

_____, and Slusser, Robert, The Theory, Law and Policy of Soviet Treaties, Stanford, Stanford University Press, 1962.

Tseng Yu-kao, The Termination of Unequal Treaties in International Law, Shanghai, The Commercial Press 1933.

Tung, William L., China and the Foreign Powers: The Impact of and Reaction to Unequal Treaties, Dobbs Ferry, N. Y., Oceana, 1970.

United Nations International Law Commission, Draft Articles on the Law of Treaties, U. N. General Assembly, Official Records, 21st Session, 1966.

United Nations Statistical Yearbook, 1950-

"United States Policy of Non-Recognition of Communist China," Department of State Bulletin, #39 (September 8, 1958).

"U.S., Red China Announce Measures for Return of Civilians," Department of State Bulletin #33 (September 19, 1955).

Vatcher, William, Panmunjon, New York, Praeger, 1958.

Vattel, E., Le Droit des gens: ou principes de la loi naturelle, (The Law of Nations or the Principles of Natural Law), Translated by C.G. Fenwick from the 1758 ed., Vol. III, Washington, D. C., Carnegie Endowment for International Peace, 1934.

Vaughn, William M., "Finding the Law of Expropriation: Traditional v. Quantitative Research," The Texas International Law Forum, Vol. II, No.2, 1966.

Vinacke, Harold M., "The Continuing Chinese Revolution," Current History, Vol. 53, No. 313, (September, 1967).

Weng, Byron S.J., Peking's U.N. Policy: Continuity and Change, New York, Praeger, 1972.

Wilson, Richard W., "The Learning of Political Symbols in Chinese Culture." Journal of Asian and African Studies, Vol. 3, Nos. 3-4, (July-October, 1968).

Wolff, Christian von, Jus gentium methodo scientifica pertratatum (The Law of Nations Treated According to a Scientific Method), Vol. II, Translated by Drake from 1764 ed., Washington, D. C., Carnegie Endowment for International Peace, 1934.

Wright, Quincy, "The Chinese Recognition Problem,"
    American Journal of International Law, Vol. 49,
    No. 3, 1955.

Wright, S.F., China's Struggle for Tariff Autonomy,
    Shanghai, Kelly Walsh, Ltd., 1938.

Yearbook of the Dutch Ministry of Foreign Affairs,
    1949-1950.

Young, Kenneth T., Negotiating with the Chinese Com-
    munists: The United States Experience, 1953-1967.
    New York, McGraw-Hill, 1968.

Yu, George T., "China's Competitive Diplomacy in Afri-
    ca," in Jerome A. Cohen, ed., The Dynamics of
    China's Foreign Relations, Harvard Asian Mono-
    graph No. 39, Harvard University Press, 1970.

Chinese Language Sources

Chao Li-hai, "The American Imperialists Trample on International Law" JMJP November 14, 1962.

Chao Yueh, "A Preliminary Criticism of Bourgeois Inter-national Law," KCWTYC, No. 3, 1959.

Cheng-fa yen-chiu, (Studies in Politics and Law), Peking, 1953-1966.

Chiao-hseuh yu yen-chiu, (Teaching and Research) Peking, 1956-1959.

Ch'ien Szu, "A Criticism of the Views of Bourgeois International Law on the Question of Population," KCWTYC, No. 5, 1960.

Ch'ien T'ai, Chung-kuo pu-p'ing teng t'iao-yueh chih yuan-ch'i chi fei-ch'u chih ching-kuo, (The Origin and Abolition of China's Unequal Treaties) Taipei, Kuo-fan yen-chiu yuan, 1961.

Chou Fu-lun, "An Inquiry into the Nature of Modern International Law," Chiao hseuh yu yen-chiu, (Teaching and Research), No. 3, Peking, March, 1958.

Chou Keng-sheng, Hsien-tai Yin-Mei kuo-chi-fa ti ssu-hsiang tung-hsiang (Trends in the thought of modern English and American International Law), Peking, Shih-chieh chih-shih ch'u-pan-she, 1963.

_____, "The Principle of Peaceful Coexistence from the Viewpoint of International Law," Cheng-fa yen-chiu, (Studies in Politics and Law), No. 6, 1955.

_____, "Refuting the Absurd Statement of the State Department of the United States," KMJP, Peking, February 7, 1956.

Chu Ch'i-wu, "Looking at the Class Character and the Succession Character of Law from the Point of View of International Law," KMJP, Peking, May 13, 1957.

Chu Li-lu, "Refuting the Absurd Theory Concerning International Law by Ch'en T'i-ch'iang," JMJP, Peking, September 18, 1957.

Chung-hua jen-min kung-ho-kuo fa-kuei hui-pien (Collection of Laws and Regulations of the People's Republic of China), 13 vols., Peking, Fa-lu ch'u-pan-she, 1956-65.

Hsin-wu, "A Criticism of Bourgeois International Law on the Question of State Territory," KCWTYC, No. 7, 1960.

K'ung Meng, "A Criticism of the Theories of Bourgeois International Law on the Subjects of International Law and the Recognition of States," KCWTYC, Vol. 2, 1960.

Kuo-chi wen-t'i yen-chiu (Studies in International Problems) Peking, Shih-chieh chih-shih ch'u-pan-she, 1956-60, 1964-1966.

Mao To, "The Important Achievements of the Conference of Afro-Asian Jurists," Cheng-fa yen-chiu (Studies in Politics and Law) No. 2, Peking, 1958.

Tan Wen-jui, "Don't Allow the Use of International Treaties as a Smoke Screen," JMJP, Peking, April 12, 1955.

Wang Yao-t'ien, Kuo-chi mao-yi t'iao-yueh ho hsieh-ting (International Trade Treaties and Agreements) Peking, T'sai-cheng ching-chi ch'u-pan-she, 1958.

Wang Yi-wang, "What is the Difference Between Commercial Treaties and Trade Agreements," KMJP, Peking, May 12, 1950.

Wei Liang, "Looking at the So-Called McMahon Line From the Viewpoint of International Law," KCWTYC, No. 6, Peking, 1960.

_____, "On Post Second World War International Treaties," KCTYC, Peking, 1961.

Ying T'ao, "A Criticism of Bourgeois International Law Concerning the Question of State Sovereignty," KCWTYC No. 3, Peking, 1960.

_____, "Recognize the True Face of Bourgeois International Law from a Few Basic Concepts," KCWTYC, No. 1, Peking, 1960.

Yu-Fan, "Speaking of the Relationship between China and the Tibetan Region from the Viewpoint of Sovereignty and Suzerainty," _JMJP,_ June 5, 1959.

Treaty Series, Collections, Computer Data Bank

Chung-hua jen-min kung-ho-kuo tui-wai kuan-hsi wen-
    chien chi, (Compilation of Documents Relating to
    the Foreign Relations of the People's Republic of
    China) Vols. I-X, Peking, Shih-chieh chih-shih
    ch'u-pan-she, 1957-65.

Chung-hua jen-min kung-ho-kuo yu-hao t'iao-yueh hui-
    pien, (Collection of Friendship Treaties of the
    People's Republic of China) Peking, Shih-chieh
    chih-shih ch'u-pan-she, 1965.

Chung-hua jen-min kung-ho-kuo t'iao-yueh chi (Collec-
    tion of treaties of the People's Republic of Chi-
    na) Vols. 1-10, Peking, Fa-lu ch'u-pan-she, 1957-
    62; Vols. 11-13, Peking, Shih-chieh chih-shih
    ch'u-pan-she, 1963-65.

Johnston, Douglas M. and Chiu, Hungdah, Agreements of
    the People's Republic of China, 1949-1967: A Cal-
    endar, Cambridge,Mass.,Harvard University Press,
    1968.

Kuo-chi t'iao-yueh chi 1953-55,(International Treaty
    Series 1953-55), Peking, Shih-chieh chih-shih
    ch'u-pan-she, 1961.

Rohn, Peter H.,Treaty Profiles,Santa Barbara,California,
    American Bibliographical Center, Clio Press, 1975.

_____, World Treaty Index, 5 vols.,Santa Barbara, Cal-
    ifornia, American Bibliographical Center, Clio
    Press, 1975.

Treaties and Agreements with and Concerning China,1919-
    1929, Carnegie Endowment for International Peace,
    Division of International Law.

Treaty Research Center, University of Washington,
    Director, Peter H. Rohn.

United States Department of State, Treaties in Force,
    Washington, D.C., 1964-66.

United States Treaties and Other International Agree-
    ments.

United Nations Treaty Series.

INDEX